DANIEL H. BURNHAM
Visionary Architect and Planner

DANIEL H. BURNHAM

Visionary Architect and Planner

Kristen Schaffer
Edited by Scott J. Tilden
Photographs by Paul Rocheleau

RIZZOLI
NEW YORK

3-16-2004
WW
$95

For Jean Liberman Seligmann —K. S.

This project has been supported by a grant from the

Graham Foundation for
Advanced Studies in the Fine Arts.

HALF TITLE PAGE
View from Union Station,
Washington, D.C.

TITLE PAGE
Grant Park, Chicago.

First published in the United States of America in 2003
by Rizzoli International Publications, Inc.
300 Park Avenue South
New York, NY 10010

© 2003 by Rizzoli International Publications, Inc.

2003 2004 2005 2006 2007/ 10 9 8 7 6 5 4 3 2 1

Printed in China
Designed by Abigail Sturges

ISBN: 0-8478-2533-7
Library of Congress Catalog Control Number: 2002115814

Contents

Acknowledgments

We wish to acknowledge the thoughtful insights and efforts of the following individuals without whose assistance this book would not have been possible.

Steven Andre, Manager, *Burnham Hotel*

Don Andreini, *San Francisco Architectural Heritage*

Martin Aurand, *Architecture Librarian and Archivist, Carnegie Mellon University*

Bruce Bradley, *Linda Hall Library of Science, Engineering and Technology*

Robert Bruegmann, *Professor of Art History, School of Architecture, University of Illinois at Chicago*

Steve Case, *Rizzoli International Publications*

Wim de Wit, *Director of Special Collections and Visual Resources, Getty Research Institute*

William Donnell, *Monadnock Building*

Zurich Esposito, *Chicago Architecture Foundation*

W. John Fuller, Sr., *Keycorp*

Wendell Garrett, *Senior Vice President, Sotheby's*

Patrick Hamilton, *Director of Engineering, Lord & Taylor*

Gunny Harboe, *McClier*

Elaine Harrington, *Chicago*

Kevin Harrington, *Professor, Lewis Department of Humanities Illinois Institute of Technology*

Jack Hartray, *Nagle Hartray Danker Kagan McKay*

Walter C. Kidney, *Pittsburgh History and Landmarks Foundation*

Laurel S. Konopski, *J. J. Gimberg Company*

Carol Herselle Krinsky, *Professor, Department of Fine Arts, New York University*

Walter E. Langsam, *Cincinnati*

Sunny Lebowitz, *Director of Publicity, Lord & Taylor*

Bonita Mall, *Chicago Architecture Foundation*

David Morton, *Rizzoli International Publications*

Caroline Nutley, *Chicago Historical Society*

Barbara Opar and Sue Miller, *Fine Arts, Byrd Library, Syracuse University*

Carl Paladino, *Ellicott Development Company*

Sarah Quail, *Graham Foundation for Advanced Studies in the Fine Arts*

John W. Reps, *Professor Emeritus, Cornell University*

Elaine Rocheleau, *Photographic services*

Renee Ross, *Engineers' Society of Western Pennsylvania*

Andrea Schwartz, *Marshall Field & Company*

Jean Seligmann, *Cortland*

Richard Solomon, *Graham Foundation for Advanced Studies in the Fine Arts*

Abigail Sturges, *Sturges Design*

Beth Sullebarger, *Executive Director of Cincinnati Preservation Association*

Albert M. Tannler, *Pittsburgh History and Landmarks Foundation*

Douglas A. Tilden, *Architect*

Margaret Webster, *Director, Visual Resources Facility, College of Architecture, Arts & Planning, Cornell University*

Mary Woolever, *Burnham Library, Art Institute of Chicago*

OPPOSITE
Marshall Field, Chicago. The Louis Comfort Tiffany glass mosaic ceiling above the south atrium is the largest in the world.

7

Preface

Scott J. Tilden

If you asked people in the know, (ca 1912) . . . to tell you who had done the most for American architecture, they would probably say that Sullivan had made some imaginative proposals and designed beautiful details, that Wright had built some interesting houses in the Middle West, that Cram's Gothic churches were excellent, that Cass Gilbert had mastered the skyscraper and Paul Cret the problem of government building, but that if you were looking for giants you had better go to New York and seek out the elegant taste and the highly developed talent of Charles Follen McKim and his partner Stanford White; they might go further and tell you that the heart of the whole enterprise lay in Chicago in the resourceful and indomitable planner, the real Titan, the emperor of architecture, "Uncle Dan" Burnham.

—John Burchard & Albert Bush-Brown
The Architecture of America: A Social and Cultural History

Unlike Burchard and Bush-Brown, few architectural historians have recognized the important architectural legacy of Chicago architect, Daniel Hudson Burnham. Before the publishing of this book, only two comprehensive books were written on Burnham's work: the excellent biography by Thomas S. Hines entitled *Burnham of Chicago: Architect and Planner* (1974) and the two volume eulogy by Charles Moore entitled *Daniel H. Burnham, Architect, Planner of Cities* (1921).

The lack of attention paid by historians to Daniel H. Burnham seems peculiar in light of his enormous contribution to the architectural field. Burnham was not only a contributor to the development of the Chicago School of Architecture and the modern skyscraper. Also an influential planner, he was the prime organizer and chief of construction for the World's Columbian Exposition of 1893, the "White City." A leader of the City Beautiful movement, Burnham developed plans for Washington, D.C., Cleveland, San Francisco, Chicago, and Manila. He was instrumental in establishing the American Academy in Rome. Burnham created one of the world's largest architectural firms, and served as a mentor to some of the young architects in his firm such as Pierce Anderson, Thomas E. Tallmadge, Dwight Perkins, William E. Drummond, and Ernest Graham.

Burnham's achievements are all the more noteworthy given his lack of formal university training in his field. He failed his entrance examinations at Harvard and Yale. These same universities conferred honorary degrees on him in 1894, the same year his admiring peers elected Burnham President of the American Institute of Architects.

Numerous reasons can be cited for the limited recognition of Burnham's importance in American architectural history. Some critics claim his first partner, John Wellborn Root, deserved the lion's share of credit for the pioneering designs. They believe that Burnham primarily secured the commissions and kept the clients contented. The negative assessments of Burnham's work by Frank Lloyd Wright and Louis Sullivan influenced the views of generations of architects and historians. Wright and Sullivan made both positive and negative comments on Burnham, but the negative ones seem to be best remembered. Most of Burnham's later works were in the Beaux-Arts style which has not met with the favor of many twentieth-century architectural critics. Architectural historian, Daniel Willis, observed, "All architectural movements direct their harshest criticisms to that which immediately precedes them. Thus Modernist critics were mostly unable to recognize the proto-Modern qualities of buildings executed in the style of the École des Beaux-Arts."[2]

OPPOSITE
Penn Station, Pittsburgh.

While it may be true that John Root designed the buildings' facades and decorative elements, Burnham interpreted the architectural needs and programs of clients and shaped the interior plans.[3] I believe that the firm's design process was a collaborative one among architects, clients, and contractors. The history of design of the Monadnock Building provides an excellent example of this process. Louis Sullivan described this building as "an amazing cliff of brickwork, rising sheer and stark, with a subtlety of line and surface, a direct singleness of purpose, that gave one the thrill of romance."[4] Was this radical design the intention from the outset of Burnham and Root?

Root's early plans for the Monadnock called for a stone base, steel-frame building, ornamentation of string courses and terracotta pier embellishments, and a tripartite facade organization. The final plans reveals

Penn Station, Pittsburgh.

a building almost completely clad with brick, unified in form, and devoid of ornament. I believe this reductionism and purity of design and materials was due more to the wishes of the clients than the architects.

In his biography of John Root, Donald Hoffmann recounts the story of how the clients, Peter and Shepherd Brooks, and their Chicago agent, Owen Aldis, dictated many of the final design elements of the Monadnock.[5] The Brooks brothers of Boston were the single largest developer of office buildings in Chicago in the 1880s. On the Monadnock building, Peter Brooks directed the architects, "My notion is to have no projecting surfaces or indentations, but to have everything flush, or flat and smooth with the walls . . . projections mean dirt, nor do they add strength to the building . . . one great nuisance (is) the lodgment of pigeons and sparrows."

Owen Aldis complained that granite was too expensive for the base, and the Brooks brothers specified that brick be used for most of the building's surface. Peter Brooks even selected the color of the brick, obsidian brown, against the objections of John Root who wanted black brick at the base then brown grading up to bright yellow at the cornice. Shepherd Brooks made the decision to revert to traditional bearing wall construction. Thus Burnham's role as leader of the "design team" of architects, clients, and contractors was crucial in the development of final building designs.

In addition to the assessments by Sullivan and Wright of Burnham, both made many positive judgments of Burnham's character. Sullivan found Burnham "a sentimentalist, a dreamer, a man of fixed determination and strong will . . . of large, wholesome, effective presence . . ."[6] Sullivan recognized Burnham as an exemplary man of the age of rising American economic and political power. Wright believed that Burnham "was not a creative architect," but he was a "great man who made masterful use of the methods and men of his time" and that as an "enthusiastic promoter of great construction enterprises . . . his powerful personality was supreme."[7]

Wright and Sullivan certainly made negative comments about Burnham the man, but their greatest objections were reserved for the style he championed, Beaux-Arts. For Burnham, the 1893 World's Columbian Exposition in Chicago was a triumph which had a lasting impact on American architecture. But it was precisely the impact of the Beaux-Arts style of the Fair on America's architectural taste which Sullivan found most distressing. Sullivan complained, "Meanwhile the virus of the World's Fair, after a period of incubation in the architectural profession and in the population at large, especially the influential, began to show unmistakable signs of the nature of contagion. There came a violent outbreak of the Classic and the Renaissance in the East which slowly spread westward, contaminating all that it touched, both at its source and outward. The damage wrought by the World's Fair will last for half a century from its date, if not longer."[8]

Wright personally admired Burnham, but his distaste for Beaux-Arts architecture is revealed in his account of Burnham's attempt to hire him in his early years. Wright relates the story, "To be brief, he would take care of my wife and children if I would go to Paris—four years of the Beaux-Arts. Then Rome—two years. Expenses all paid. A job with him when I got back. It was more than merely generous. It was splendid. But I was frightened. I was embarrassed not knowing what to say." Wright thanked Burnham and declined the offer saying, "I am spoiled already, I've been too close to Mr. Sullivan. He has helped . . . spoil me for the Beaux-Arts."

Sullivan's and Wright's distaste for the Fair's architectural influence and the Beaux-Arts style was shared by many architectural historians of the first half of the twentieth century. Sigfried Gidion stated, "American architecture was (being) undermined by the most dangerous reaction since its origins."[9] James Marston Fitch thought the rise of Beaux-Arts architecture was due to America's "failing esthetic standards."[10] Montgomery Schuyler was more subtle in his criticism. He had "hearty admiration for the Fair and its builders." It was a "festal and temporary vision of beauty" but not a real, living, and progressive American architecture characterized by a correlation between structure and function. "Arcadian architecture is one thing and American architecture is another."[11] Lewis Mumford lamented the Fair's spawning of the City Beautiful movement in which the Beaux-Arts style was used as a "municipal cosmetic" to create "imperial facades" in countless American cities.[12]

Continental and Commercial National Bank (now 208 South LaSalle Building), Chicago.

With the rise of postmodernism and later architecture, many historians have developed a greater openness to classicism, historicism and eclectic styles and hopefully an enhanced regard for the work of Daniel H. Burnham. I believe a greater appreciation of Burnham's important architectural legacy will also be fostered by the writings of Dr. Kristen Schaffer and the photographs of Paul Rocheleau in this book. Dr. Schaffer provides a fresh perspective on Burnham. She reassesses his role in his partnership with John Root, explores his impact on the business and practice of architecture, and analyzes his interest in the provision and planning of public space. Mr. Rocheleau captures beautiful images of Burnham's buildings, parks, and elements of his city plans. Together, Schaffer and Rocheleau refocus attention on Burnham's architectural achievements and influence, illuminating the complexities of practice at the turn of nineteenth-century America.

11

Introduction

The Architect and Chicago

The city of Chicago developed rapidly during the second half of the nineteenth century. In that time, the modest town just a few decades old exploded into the second-largest American city with over a million and a half inhabitants. The city lay at the juxtaposition of the two vast waterway systems of North America. Located on Lake Michigan, the city had access to the Atlantic Ocean by way of the Great Lakes, the miracle of the Erie Canal, and the Hudson River. Or, by moving upstream on the Chicago River and over a relatively short portage to the Des Plaines and on to the Illinois, the city was accessible to the entire Mississippi River Basin, the heartland of the United States, and ultimately downriver to the Gulf of Mexico. The construction of canals reinforced this natural advantage by making the Illinois waterway link complete. And when the city became the hub of the nation's railroad system, Chicago solidified its place at the crossroads of U.S. agricultural production and the rest of the world.

The city grew big and talked big (hence the nickname "the Windy City") and it is in this setting that Daniel Hudson Burnham faced the challenge of creating an architectural practice that matched the energy and the demands of the city[1] (fig. 1).

Burnham was up to that challenge. "Uncle Dan" to the architectural community, he was a larger-than-life figure in this city of great feats and expectations. The vigorous commercial metropolis was an essential factor in the making of Burnham and in understanding his contribution to the architecture that it spawned. Once he had decided on architecture as his career, Burnham dedicated himself, as he said, "to try to become the greatest architect in the city or the country." He accepted no less, and thought he would be able to achieve his goal through a "determined and persistent effort."[2] For nearly half a century, Burnham was the head of one of the world's most prominent architectural practices, and was recognized as the preeminent urban planner of his generation.

Earlier, in the years 1873 to 1891, Burnham and John Wellborn Root had built one of the most successful architectural practices, critically and financially, in the United States. They began their careers designing residences, but from the outset Burnham strove for larger projects: "my idea is to work up a big business, to handle big things, deal with big businessmen, and to build up a big organization, for you can't handle big things unless you have an organization." In fact, the business corporation was the model for the large architectural offices that arose at the same time. Not intending any flattery, Louis H. Sullivan observed that "the only architect in Chicago to catch the significance of this movement was Daniel Burnham, for in its tendencies toward bigness, organization, delegation and intense commercialism, he sensed the reciprocal workings of his own mind." Casting this same trait in a different light, a former employee recalled that "Burnham was one of the first architects to build up a highly efficient and well-equipped office organization to satisfy the needs of a rapidly increasing business." Burnham engineered the transition to the modern large architectural practice.[3]

Forging such a practice was a sensible, perhaps necessary, reaction to changes in architecture, especially in Chicago. The city's rapid development, coupled with a circumscribed downtown (limited by Lake Michigan on the east, branches of the Chicago River on the north and west, and a bulwark of railroad yards on the south), put extraordinary pressure on land values. It promoted the construction of the tall commercial buildings that were becoming technologically feasible by developments in steel structural systems; in fireproofing and sanitation; and in the safety, reliabil-

ity, and speed of the elevator. These new buildings were unprecedented not only in their height but also in their complexity, taxing the abilities of architects and causing the transformation of architectural practice. Burnham and Root achieved success by exploring and pioneering both the appearance and the requirements of this new building type. They designed some of the earliest skyscrapers in the world and in the process learned much about their planning and economics.

Tall speculative office buildings produced significant revenue for investors. The more quickly architects and contractors designed and constructed a building, the sooner it could begin to realize a return. Time as well as space was money.[4] Such large-scale speculative office buildings marked an important change in architectural history. Up until the industrial revolution, architects had focused their attention on prominent symbolic structures such as churches, palaces, and government buildings. Since that time commercial buildings had become increasingly more significant, so that by the end of the nineteenth century revenue-producing tall office buildings were among the most substantial commissions architects could receive. And if architects were to flourish in this new climate, one thing became clear: the architect of the skyscraper could not be the romanticized individual artist. The artistic aspect of design had to become one of a number of concerns for architects practicing in large American cities. This was not unique to Chicago. As one East Coast architect observed: "In our art the productions of the individual have been supplanted. It now takes several men to make a good architect." Increasingly architects became members of large and diverse design and construction teams that included clients, clients' agents, contractors, draughtsmen and detailers, specification writers, various engineers, job superintendents, manufacturers and suppliers, to say nothing of laborers. Collaborating with numerous participants from outside the profession, architects worked to maintain a dominant role on this expanded design team.[5]

Burnham maintained dominance, leading with the force of his personality as well as with the organizational skills he had developed. Colleagues remarked that he "inspired confidence" and had a "powerful and positive personality." As Sullivan observed, he

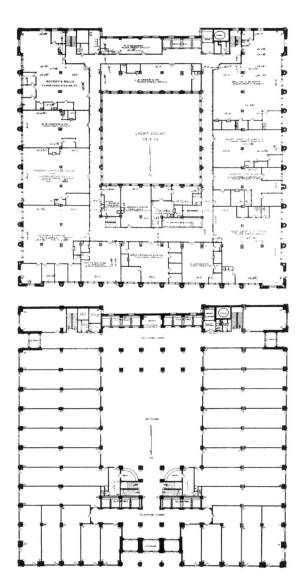

Fig. 2. Insurance Exchange, Chicago. Typical and first floor plans. A late example (1911–1912) of the plan type favored by Burnham.

was "a man of fixed determination and strong will—no doubt about that." He had both the project and the office under tight control, and he conveyed that to both clients and employees. In the early years of practice, Burnham had learned the value of good organization. He once advised a young employee to

> study the organization side of business . . . don't you know that you can hire any number of civil engineers, mechanical engineers and electrical engineers who will be absolutely contented to spend their whole lives in doing routine?

Burnham was able to have his hand in any aspect of any project in the office because he would oversee all the work while delegating most of the actual tasks: "The only way to handle a big business is to delegate, delegate, delegate."[6]

The orchestration of the design team and the delegation of work in the office, both under his close oversight, combined with his strong leadership, led contemporaries to extol Burnham's administrative ability. Because of this Burnham is often, and simplistically, characterized as the "business" partner in the firm. Since he handled the office affairs and dealt with the clients, this appraisal is to some extent true. But that was not all he did. In addition to his "power of organization and administration," fellow architects also praised his "unerring discernment of the client's needs." This ability, of grasping the client's requirements, directly relates to the planning of a building. Contemporaries called this planning talent "administrative ability" too, and this has caused considerable confusion about Burnham's role in the office.[7]

To be clear, in addition to his business and client responsibilities, Burnham generally laid out the building's plan, taking into careful consideration the satisfaction of functional and economic requirements. Burnham typically did not design the facades of the firm's buildings but he planned most of them, as a fellow architect made clear:

> When a man has no time to make large drawings, he has to make small ones, and he has to reduce the size of his sheets of paper as the demands on his time increase. That is what Burnham did. He could lay out the plan for a large building on sheets six inches square; and he would not only make one plan, but would use sheets enough to lay it out according to every arrangement he could conceive of until he found the best one to recommend to his client. That is what I have seen him do.

Fig. 3. The Rookery, Chicago. The necessary stair from the balcony to the third floor becomes a spectacular event.

Burnham had the "capacity to produce a scheme in planning that would prove to be a good paying investment," and was said to have had a "positive genius" for making buildings yield revenue[8] (fig. 2).

By having command of the plan, Burnham more firmly established his leadership over the design team. He took control of the project through the act of planning, as one of his employees observed:

> He considered it his first duty to permit the structure to serve in the most economical manner possible the combination of functions for which it was intended. In planning he was confronted by a problem the difficulty of which was equalled only by its importance, and if he had

not shown himself equal to the task he would have become eventually the subordinate of the building engineers who played such an important part in the evolution of the skyscraper. That he retained his pre-eminence during this period of structural revolution in spite of the increasing importance of the purely engineering and practical problems involved is adequate indication that he performed his task efficiently . . . He possessed precisely the kind of ability required to meet these new conditions.

With increased complexity and so many professionals involved, there was a greater compartmentalization of tasks and team members often saw only one piece of a project. Burnham maintained the unity of the entire design through control of the process and supervision of all the parts. Unfortunately, misunderstandings about this role, in addition to the confusion over the term administrative ability, have denigrated Burnham's part in the production of the firm's buildings; and with that Burnham has been denied the status of "designer."[9]

Architects, historians, and critics have often overlooked the importance of economics as a planning problem to be solved by the architect in a revenue-producing building. Most focus on the building's facade, and they designate the architect who designed it as "the designer" of the building. Even when function is considered, the expression of function is emphasized over the actual satisfaction of functional criteria. For instance, in the article where he presents his famous "form ever follows function" formulation, Sullivan discusses function mostly in terms of how to artistically and ornamentally represent it on the facade. In fact, in most firms the architect described as the designer was the architect who composed facades and ornamented construction. By today's standards, however, conceiving and developing the building's plan constitutes architecture as much as the composition and decoration of the vertical surface. Burnham was a designer of the firm's buildings but his contribution has been misunderstood; his "administrative ability" was thought to apply only to the running of the office and not to his talent as the building's planner.[10]

For Burnham, however, it all was one, all part of a single process and intent, all part of the design. All his skills and resources were aimed at delivering the best

OPPOSITE
Fig. 4. Ellicott Square Building, Buffalo. One of two atrium stairs that links the major public space with the balcony.

Fig. 5. Railway Exchange, Chicago. Grand stair to the balcony.

building he could, and all this was noted at the time. Burnham "had a feeling for all those elements which tend to lift a structure out of the category of mere profit-yielders, and make it an ornament to a city" (figs. 3 and 4). He could convince his client that it was economically feasible, indeed advisable, to spend "large sums of money for the assumed aesthetic appearance of his building." He was able to make the client "appreciate that attractiveness in general design adds materially to the revenue productiveness of his enterprise" (fig. 5). Burnham's buildings "set a standard of equipment and finish that actually created a public demand for high class commercial buildings which fairly forced the owner to meet this demand" (figs. 6 and 7). Or as another contemporary put it: "It was through Burnham's great energy and ability to educate his own clients that so much of this work came to his firm."[11]

Burnham possessed both a "faculty for analysis and plan" and a "poetic conception of what was fittest." And like Root, he aspired to "pure architecture" in their commercial work. He had a sense of what was to

17

be accomplished, a vision of the project's possibilities. After all, what was the use of notable business acumen and organizational skills if there were no worthy goal, no passion for architecture driving him? It is Burnham's duality as organizer and artist, practical man of affairs and dreamer, and a visionary with sound business judgement, that seems to account for his success:

> He was never so much of a businessman that he was not also an artist. He felt as an artist, thought as an artist, and when he came up against his limitations in knowledge or as a creator, he never failed to recognize those qualities in others.

His friends and colleagues recalled "his love for everything beautiful." Even Frank Lloyd Wright remarked that Burnham "loved the beautiful and served it." Sullivan called Burnham:

> a sentimentalist, a dreamer . . . a man who readily opened his heart if one were sympathetic . . . He averred that romance need not die out; that there must still be joy to the soul in doing big things in a big personal way, devoid of the sordid.

Burnham had faith in the transcendent power of beauty. It informed his idealism and belief that his art had potential for human good. This largeness of spirit and sense of endless possibilities found expression in his dedication to public service, which he believed was his duty.[12]

The aspects of public service, beauty, and the importance of the plan came together in Burnham's city planning work. Almost all of his city plans were done as public service, offering his time and expertise without compensation. Burnham's organizational skill allowed him to delegate office projects so that he could devote himself to city planning. His success as a planner of commercial buildings contributed to his belief that a good city plan could also have financial advantages. He advocated city planning as a sound economic strategy. Profitability was not the only benefit of planning, nor was it satisfactory by itself for Burnham. The plan also provided organic unity and in itself was able to embody beauty. Burnham's commitment to city planning as an act of architecture is evident in his belief in the beauty of the plan. He was an architect who believed in the necessity of training in architecture before undertaking city planning.[13]

As a part of what is known as the "City Beautiful" movement, Burnham has suffered a curious reversal

Fig. 8. Grant Park, Chicago. Although developed after his death, the park's design reflects Burnham's intention for beautiful structures and formal green spaces.

of fate (fig. 8). Instead of being characterized as all business and administration, here historians and critics have accused him of engaging in a superficial striving for beauty without proper consideration of practical matters. This is as much of a distortion as saying that in his architecture he had no role in design. The consistency of Burnham's career is that in both architecture and city planning he was involved in all aspects of design, he was concerned with both function and beauty, and he was most directly and consistently involved with planning. Burnham saw it all as one process, where the artistic solution was integrally related with the practical one. And the two were related through the vehicle of the plan.

Burnham invested his city plans with mystical significance as well as beauty. He was a member of the Church of the New Jerusalem founded by Emanuel Swedenborg, an eighteenth-century mystic who described a correspondence between the physical and heavenly realms. Swedenborg's teachings permitted

Burnham to see the city plan as an inscription of cosmic import, a representation of heavenly order. His faith led him to believe as well that the study of architecture was the "striving after the beautiful and useful laws God has created to govern his material universe," and that such study could "open the mind more and more to the Great Architect of the Universe." His religious creed also encouraged him to dedicate himself to the public good and to public service. One of its tenets was to make oneself useful to society. A close friend and fellow Swedenborgian saw in their Church's "conception of Charity . . . as the love of the neighbor" the inspiration for Burnham's professional life and work.[14]

Burnham was a Swedenborgian from childhood. Born in Henderson, New York, in 1846, he spent his early childhood gazing westward down the length of Lake Ontario. In 1855, he moved with his parents to Chicago, where he grew and matured with the city.

The Early Years:
After the Great Fire
and before the
World's Fair

Burnham announced to his mother that he would become an architect in 1867. He was filled with ambition and determination, but the early years of his career were not easy or steady ones. And failure had precipitated its choice. Burnham had wanted to attend Harvard University. Between 1863 and 1867, he studied in Massachusetts, first at a preparatory school and then with private tutors. But he failed the admission examination to Harvard, and to Yale too, and returned to Chicago. His studies, however, introduced him to architecture and its history, and Burnham lit upon architecture as a career, at first inconsistently despite the assured declaration to his mother.[1]

Late in 1867 he entered the firm of Loring and Jenney, where he remained for just one year. Still not completely committed to architecture, he left Chicago. He returned in December 1870, and worked at a number of different jobs. It was not until 1872 that Burnham found fulfillment in architecture. In that year his father found him a position in the firm of Carter, Drake and Wight, where he was under Peter B. Wight's "personal direction as a student." Like most practitioners of his time, Burnham learned his profession as an apprentice in an architectural office, without academic training. No schools of architecture existed in the United States until 1868. Unlike Richard Morris Hunt or H. H. Richardson, Burnham did not attend the École des Beaux-Arts in Paris.[2]

Burnham met John W. Root in Carter, Drake and Wight's office, where Root was chief draftsman. Born in 1850 in Georgia, Root had studied in Liverpool, England, during the American Civil War, and after returning to the United States had earned a degree in civil engineering at New York University. He had worked in New York City for James Renwick and J. B. Snook, and had interviewed with Wight while Wight was still practicing in New York. When Wight moved to Chicago to take advantage of the building boom after the fire, Root followed there in January 1872. That Burnham, a student in the office, was able to convince the head draftsman with a university education to leave his steady job and go into partnership with him says much about Burnham's power of persuasion and his ability to inspire confidence.[3]

Burnham and Root formed their architectural partnership at an inauspicious moment. They began practice in Chicago a couple of years after the great fire but just months before the financial panic of 1873, thereby missing most of the post-fire construction boom. The two partners managed to survive by hiring themselves out to better established firms and by taking odd jobs. Despite this difficult beginning, their practice would grow with the vitality of the city.

The synergy of Burnham and Root's partnership was the source of their success, as they reinforced, balanced, and encouraged each other. They had complementary personalities: Burnham was all solidity and strength, Root all "brilliancy and color and swiftness." As an acquaintance described them, together they appeared as "some big strong tree with the lightning playing around it." Relatives, friends, employees, and biographers have all noted the reciprocity of character traits that enabled the two to form not only an enduring partnership, but an intimate friendship as well. Both partnership and friendship endured the difficulties of practice, lasting solidly until Root's death in 1891.[4]

Of the two, Root possessed greater facility in the design of facades and the development of ornament. However, he lacked the focus and determination of his partner. As a young man, family members feared he was in "danger of dilettanteism [sic]." Louis H. Sullivan thought Root had not "one tenth of his partner's settled will, nor of said partner's capacity to go through hell to reach an end." But Root had "great versatility and restrained originality" as a designer. It was over these qualities which

> Burnham enthused with all the exuberance of unrestrained enthusiasm. It was this which caused the business to increase, for Burnham never let an occasion pass without proclaiming the great talents of his partner. It was one of the secrets of their success. Also it relieved Root from any necessity of blowing his own trumpet.

Burnham shielded Root from clients and problems; but this too contributed to the perception that Root did all the designing and that Burnham did none.[5]

Root was also responsible for structural design, but here he functioned more like Burnham in that he delegated the details. Root's "mathematical and engineering abilities were deficient," but his judgement was "the quickest and best." Root had to consult engineers to realize his designs, yet he was able to "suggest to a specialist an idea which would illuminate him, and enable him to work out a solution to a hard problem in a new and brilliant manner."[6]

Burnham did indeed handle clients and the business, and he too had a role in design. He laid out most of the buildings the firm produced with an eye toward functional efficiency and economic return. In doing this, he also established the building's concept by indicating a particular strategy or choosing a plan type.

In her biography of her brother-in-law, Harriet Monroe waxed enthusiastic over Root's abilities as a designer and constructive engineer, focusing on his achievements. But she did not fail to acknowledge Burnham's role, and gave him credit for his contribution to the design process. She described Burnham as a "very suggestive" critic for Root (the importance of which should not be underestimated in any partnership) and as the building planner:

> Mr. Burnham was skillful in laying out a building. Mr. Root did not enjoy this part of the work, and rarely assumed it, except in the case of buildings which presented novel planning problems, or in which he felt a special loving interest, such as the Art Institute, the Women's Temple and many residences. When a building came to the office, Mr. Burnham, as a rule, laid out more or less roughly ground and floor plans. Frequently, he made many such studies, the partners deciding together upon the best one, which Root would use as the first element of his problem in designing the exterior.[7]

Root's plans were sometimes less than successful. For instance, the Art Institute Building was criticized by a contemporary writer who "thought the rooms had been obliged to work themselves out for the sake of the elevations."[8] Occasionally, Burnham did sketches of the building's elevation. Monroe listed buildings in which Burnham "claims a share, by virtue of rough sketches embodying the starting point of an idea," saying that in some cases the "relationship between his suggestion and the final design was slight, while in those of the Monadnock and the First Regiment Armory it was closest."[9] These two buildings were among the firm's simplest and most compelling.

Monroe was not the only one to note Burnham's involvement. Wight observed that Burnham used to make a great many "rapid sketches," impressing the client with the ability of the firm to "solve any problem." Most often these sketches were "afterward elaborated by Root with the greatest care." Given this evidence, it is most likely that the two worked together in real partnership on their commissions. A building's design was jointly theirs, with each partner contributing to the outcome. Generally, Root worked out Burnham's plan, and Burnham criticized Root's facade, although sometimes Root laid out the building and Burnham sketched an elevation. This book seeks not to discredit Root nor minimize his talents as a designer. Rather, it intends to recognize Burnham's ability as a planner, often overlooked but evinced by

Fig. 10. Union Stock Yards Gate, Chicago. With the Stockyards demolished, the gate exists as an isolated artifact.

the success of the firm in planning and designing commercial office buildings after Root's death, and by Burnham's own career as a city planner.[10]

Burnham and Root's first projects were almost all residences, sometimes including a barn. They designed houses for Chicago's well-to-do on the south side of the city, and one, on the elite residential street of Prairie Avenue, proved to be unusually important for Burnham. In 1874, John Sherman, co-founder of the Chicago Union Stockyards, retained the firm to design his new home. This commission led to Burnham's marriage to Sherman's daughter Margaret, which gave Burnham access to wealthier social circles of the city. In 1879, the firm designed a house for James M. Walker, president of the Union Stockyard and Transit Company, and general solicitor of the Chicago, Burlington and Quincy Railroad. This time it was Root who married the client's daughter, Mary Louise. Both marriages led to many opportunities for

the firm, including commissions for the entry gate and offices for the stockyards[11] (fig. 10).

In 1880, the firm received its first major commission for an office building, the functional type that would establish its reputation. The Grannis Block (1880–81) was a seven-story brick and terracotta office building in the Loop, the heart of Chicago's central business district.[12] The use of brick instead of stone on a large commercial building was a significant and recent development. William LeBaron Jenney promoted brick and terracotta as more fire resistant and less expensive than stone, and had first used these materials on his nearby Portland Block (1872). Burnham and Root followed this lead in materials but with a difference. As Burnham would later boast:

> Here our originality began to show. We made the front of the building all red, the terracotta exactly matching the brick. It was a wonder. Everyone went to see it and the town was proud of it.

23

Burnham and Root located their office in the Grannis upon its completion.[13]

The Grannis Building was significant in the career of Burnham and Root for three other reasons. It was the first time the partners worked with either Peter or Shepherd Brooks, speculators in Chicago real estate who would give the firm a number of commissions. The architects organized the Grannis around a light court, an element that they would use later to develop a distinctive commercial plan type. The architects also attempted a sectional arrangement in which the first two floors are both prime or "first" floors (here a tall banking floor over low storefronts). They would develop this strategy over time to become a significant aspect of the tall office building.[14]

Fire tested the Grannis in 1885. Its structure of load-bearing walls and terracotta covered cast iron columns survived, and the building was renovated. However, the fire damaged Burnham and Root's office, destroying all their drawings save those in progress which were stored in a vault. After the fire, the partners moved their office into another building they had recently designed, the Montauk Block.[15]

The ten-story Montauk (1881–82) "soared" over the Loop's four to six-story buildings. With its unprecedented height, two elevators, and 150 offices, the building earned the title of the first skyscraper in Chicago. An architectural historian has identified it as "the first large commercial project . . . in the new scientific spirit," where "all the factors involved" in the building type were analyzed, such as "the economic need, the costs, the financial possibilities, and the utilitarian requirements" as well as "the technical means" to meet the demands of the project. Peter Brooks commissioned the Montauk and dictated its design features.[16]

Brooks specified a plain, face-brick building with no projections to catch dirt, and minimal use of terracotta and stone: "The building throughout is to be for use and not for ornament. Its beauty will be in its all-adaptation to its use." He knew just what could be represented as selling points without ornament:

> The brick arch over the main entrance might be carried in several feet over the vestibule and inside steps to . . . convey the idea of strength. Indeed all the entries might be of face brick . . . which would convey the idea of 'fireproof' to the whole structure—a valuable idea in a [tall] building.

Responding to the architects' proposals he acknowledged that the "most is certainly made of the lot, to the credit of the architects," but was not sure that "it can be built well for the sum proposed." He complained of its extravagance: "The architects are of course indifferent to the future cost of repairs and care, an item worthy of much consideration." The architects were not permitted to remain indifferent for long. Working with Peter Brooks, Burnham learned much about client priorities and the centrality of economics in design. That the most had been made of the lot, even by Brooks's standard, was praise for the economy of the plan.[17]

The Montauk Block had a hybrid structure; exterior load-bearing walls with interior cast iron columns and wrought iron beams encased in tile to make them largely fireproof. The design of the building evinces another attempt to create two prime floors. The ground floor was a "high" basement, that is, just a few steps down from street level, with a *piano nobile* above.[18] The building was remarkably plain, and although at the time understood to be important, it was not necessarily well liked. In fact, when a prospective client called on the firm he admitted that, while admiring most of the firm's work, he did not like the Montauk Block. Root shocked him by responding, "Who in hell does?" The architects struggled with the expression of the skyscraper as well as with technical and planning problems. Nevertheless, the Montauk exemplified a distinguishing characteristic of Chicago architecture. New York architectural critic Montgomery Schuyler recognized the "very great share" Chicago businessmen had in the "evolution of commercial architecture" there, through the insistence on accepting functional and economic requirements.[19]

In the next few years, Burnham and Root designed the six-story Chicago, Burlington, and Quincy Railroad General Office (1882–83); the seven-story Traders Building (1884–85); the ten-story Counselman (1883–84); and the Calumet (1882–84), Rialto (1883–86), Insurance Exchange (1884–85), and Phenix (1885–87) buildings, all nine stories. These commissions, all in Chicago, constituted a remarkable body of tall buildings in a short time. And by the mid-1880s, Burnham and Root had added stores, railroad stations, apartments, club houses, hotels, and banks to the list of buildings they had designed, as well as the McCormick Offices and Warehouse (1884–86), and the Art Institute Building (1885–87) (fig. 11).

By designing functional skyscrapers, the firm made its name and its profits. Clients hired Burnham and Root to design buildings that made money, the importance of which was made clear by an architectural writer of the era:

> Current American architecture is not a matter of art, but of business. A building must pay or there will be no investor ready with the money to meet its cost. This is at once the curse and the glory of American architecture.

Schuyler described how "in this strictly utilitarian building the requirements are imposed with a stringency elsewhere unknown in the same degree," and opined it was "very greatly to the advantage of the architecture." Yet the tall office building could not remain strictly utilitarian if it were to be the home of white collar workers who thought themselves cultured and civilized, or of businesses with status aspirations.[20]

Burnham and Root had the benefit of working with Peter and Shepherd Brooks's real estate agent, Owen Aldis. Aldis was, of course, knowledgeable about the cost effectiveness of a plan, square footage returns, and the price of maintenance and upkeep. But he also knew that such a focus on economics would not be enough to attract the best tenants. Aldis developed the fundamental criteria of office building design from the point of view of profitable economic return by emphasizing "good light and air, attractive lobbies and corridors, easy circulation, and good building service and maintenance." Aldis advocated high-quality interiors, and tenants began to clamor for them. Perhaps in reaction to the bald speculative quality of the Montauk, ornamentation as well as good quality materials and finishes were demanded for buildings of the first-class rental category. There was a recognized commercial value to beauty; the economic problem needed an artistic solution.[21]

Tenants required adequate sunlight and fresh air in rented offices. A major planning problem for skyscrapers, the penetration of sunlight into interior work spaces limited office depth and arrangement. Given standard floor-to-ceiling heights of ten to twelve feet, the maximum depth from exterior win-

dow to corridor wall ranged between twenty and twenty-eight feet. Generally divided in two, the office with exterior windows was the private space for the principal or manager. The interior office, for the stenographer or other staff, borrowed light from the exterior office through glazed panels, either transparent or translucent, and air through operable transoms. Similar panels and transoms in turn helped to light and ventilate the public corridor, which was also frequently lit by windows in the elevator shaft behind open-cage elevators. If the building site were narrow, the rental space might be only a single office deep between exterior wall and corridor. If the building site were deep, double offices could be located on both sides of the corridor, up to the maximum depth.

Fig. 11. Art Institute Building, Chicago. Later the Chicago Club (demolished).

The Rookery
Chicago

Fig. 12. Historical photo of the light court showing the original design and details.

Although a new technological wonder made possible by gas and later electrical lights, and by mechanical heating and sometimes cooling systems, the tall office building still relied heavily on natural light and air.[22]

Burnham solved the lighting and ventilation problem in the Chicago, Burlington, and Quincy (CB&Q) Railroad General Office Building (1882–83) by employing an ancient plan type. The hollow square or square donut configuration was formed by a zone of rooms surrounding a central open space. This plan type had a long history in Western architecture, having been used throughout the Mediterranean and Middle East. Buildings as functional as the *caravanserai* or as symbolic as the palazzo employed it.[23] Burnham used it in this corporate commission, in a way more appropriate to Chicago's climate. The large central space, which rose up through all six floors of the CB&Q Building, was covered at the top by a huge iron and glass roof. Improvements in the ferro-vitreous skylight made possible this light-filled, large-span

space. Arranged around the periphery, offices opened onto galleries that ringed the court, gaining light and ventilation from interior glass doorways and transoms as well as exterior windows. The light court also provided circulation space, with stairs, elevators, and galleries open to view. A large, interior public space of movement and vitality, this solution to the functional problems of light and air also had spatial, aesthetic, and social import. With clarity of organization, the court provided a dynamic space. The light, bright open space gave the building identity. And the civilized, clean interior provided a haven from the dirty, sooty, chaotic street.[24]

Burnham and Root's Phenix Insurance Company Building (1885–87) possessed an exterior light court that was simply a functional solution. The long, shallow indentation at the rear of this narrow building created just a sliver of a light well. Of greater interest is the construction of that light well wall. Non-bearing, this thin wall of glazed brick hung from the skele-

26

tal structure permitting large window openings. Its thinness contradicted the dominant aesthetic of weighty monumentality that imparted a sense of permanence and solidity to buildings. Here the architects employed this structural innovation where it could not readily be seen from the street. Yet the thinness, the openness, and the ability to use light, reflective, non-bearing materials made possible by this innovation were ideally suited to light courts.[25]

Both the CB&Q and Phenix were important antecedents for the Rookery (1885–88), one of the firm's largest and most successful buildings (fig. 9). Many of the firm's works read, in hindsight, as more tentative efforts when compared to the Rookery. Occupying a full quarter of one of Chicago's large square city blocks, the building was configured as a hollow square with a light court occupying the center (figs. 12 and 16). Even though the Rookery was not the first interior light court building, its clarity of organization and simplicity of plan granted it a compelling primacy (figs. 13 and 14). The legibility of the ancient plan type, revitalized to meet the needs of the speculative office building, was the source of its power.[26]

With eleven stories accommodating over 600 offices, the Rookery was the largest office building in Chicago. Burnham's childhood friend, businessman Edward C. Waller, arranged a ninety-nine year lease of the land from the city for his clients, the Brooks brothers and Aldis.[27] Burnham probably developed the plan with advice from Waller,[28] and it became evident almost immediately that the plan was the source of the Rookery's success. Contemporary critic Schuyler observed that the Rookery was

> not artistically so successful, either in mass or in detail, as some other buildings of the firm, but at the same time it was built it was, perhaps, the most impressive of all by dint of the Roman largeness of its plan and the thoroughness with which it was carried out to the last detail, as a matter not alone or mainly of artistic elaboration, but of practical administration.

Schuyler evinced an appreciation of Burnham's planning ability, but he distinguished the efficacy and the elegance of the plan from the aesthetic aspect of design. He remarked that the interior was "impressive . . . by the faculty of planning that it displays, by the practical satisfaction of the practical requirements, by the administrative faculty." When he spoke of the artistic aspect, Schuyler limited himself to the vertical surface and ornamentation. Here again the conceptualization of spatial arrangements as an architectural problem-solving ability was denied artistic status as Schuyler made the distinction between "artistic elaboration" and "practical administration."[29]

Schuyler's "Roman largeness" well characterized the spaciousness of the first floor plan and section of the Rookery. The clients and architects strove not for the most economical solution in the meanest terms, but for something grander and more monumental that would yield higher revenues. The Rookery

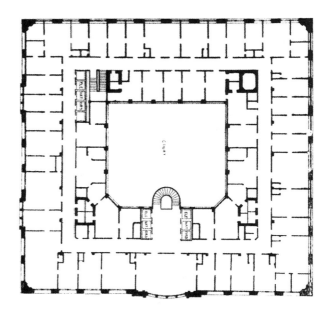

Fig. 13. Typical floor plan of original design.

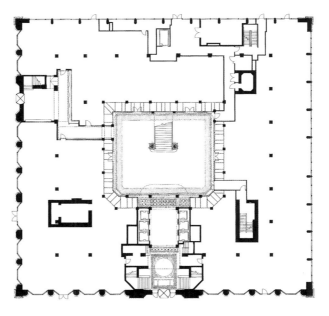

Fig. 14. Restored first floor plan.

The Rookery
Chicago

Fig. 15. Stairs from the
second floor balcony to
the third floor. The open
metal work risers con-
tribute to the lightness
of the stairs.

RIGHT
Fig. 16. Light court, with
Frank Lloyd Wright's
renovations, looking
northeast.

OPPOSITE
Fig. 19. An original iron column, underneath later cladding, is now exposed.

OVERLEAF
Fig. 20. The light court looking southwest. The stairs to the balcony are on axis with the entrance through the elevator lobby.

The Rookery
Chicago

Fig. 17. The low-ceilinged elevator lobby between the vestibule and the light court.

RIGHT
Fig. 18. The vestibule as renovated by Wright. Originally the balustrades were pierced and the balcony gently curving.

30

contained a considerable amount of "wasted" (that is to say, non-rentable) public space. Yet this unoccupied space had another function. Representative of decorum and status, space became an indicator of a building's place within the hierarchy of the city's structures.[30]

The Rookery's well-developed spatial sequence of varying height and width is a marker of the building's and, by association, the tenants' class status. The generous, arched entrance opens into a two-story vestibule with flanking stairways to the second floor (fig. 18). On axis with the entrance is the narrowed, lowered passage that acts as the lobby for the flanking banks of elevators (fig. 17). The elevator lobby widens slightly at the far end, permitting diagonal views in anticipation of the destination, the building's central light court. Here is a well-choreographed sequence of compression and then release into the spatial and visual expansion of the two-and-a-half story light court or atrium.

Balconies ring the atrium at the second level and just above, the whole is covered with an iron and glass roof. Sunlight penetrates the open center of the building into this major public space. The interior finishes are highly reflective, especially the mosaic tile floor. The original open metal work of the railings and thin iron columns allowed light to find its way into every corner (fig. 19). The stair to the balconies once had open metalwork risers. This stair, placed on axis with the entrance, led to the second floor balcony which functioned as something of a pedestrian streetfront here on the interior. Desirable by virtue of its location on this major public space, the mezzanine acted as a second "prime" floor, adding to the ground floor shops which were accessible from both the court and exterior streets.[31]

The Rookery's attractiveness came not only from the "Roman largeness of its plan" but also from "the thoroughness with which it was carried out to the last detail," and here Root's design ability is displayed. Not only in reflective surfaces and openness of details that reinforced the sense of movement and the liveliness of the space, Root's talent is exhibited in the resolution of the sequence of movement. From the unique public space to the repetitive floors above, there is a spectacular transition (fig. 20). At the top of the atrium stair, the balconies double back on each

side, meeting just above the point of entry into the space. Then in one last grand gesture, symmetrical flights of stairs cantilever out over the space from each balcony, then turn and join mid-air into a single axial stair which disappears through the skylight to the third floor. There the stair resolves itself into a single helix, rising up the full height of the building in an oriel that overlooks the open air light well above the skylight (fig. 15). This grandly theatrical gesture has been likened to the work of Piranesi, a complete set of whose prints the firm owned. This dramatic interior is one of the best examples of the two partners working together, each contributing to the architectural quality of the outcome.[32]

Above the atrium skylight was the open light well and air shaft that occupied the hollow center of the building (fig. 21). The surrounding upper floors each contained a double ring of offices opening off the continuous corridor; the "outside" offices having windows on the exterior of the building, the "inside" offices on the court. This double-loaded racetrack corridor configuration provided every office direct access to light and air, and permitted use of almost the entire block.[33]

The interior light court of the Rookery was made possible by the same structural system as that utilized in the Phenix Building.[34] An independent metal skeleton supports the wall of the Rookery's light well. Large windows take up almost two-thirds of the surface. The remaining wall consists of rather narrow continuous spandrels, upon which sit modestly sized piers. Both are constructed of glazed, white brick to reflect as much light as possible and (it was hoped) to wash clean in the rain. The wall surface is plain, adorned with a simple line of terracotta ornament on the continuous window headers. The overall effect is open and horizontal, with layers of windows upon layers of spandrels, layer upon horizontal layer, simple and repetitive.[35]

The light well walls differ profoundly from the exterior of the building (fig. 22). The facade consists of a load-bearing granite base, with polished red-granite columns, and obsidian brick and terracotta above, behind which is a metal frame. Constructed during the transition from masonry to metal skeletal structure, the Rookery employs both systems.[36] Burnham, however, wanted to use only the skeletal con-

struction on the exterior as well as the interior court, which would have allowed for larger openings. Root reportedly convinced the client to choose the heavier wall articulation.[37]

On the exterior, floor heights and window openings vary so much that they seem arbitrarily sized and shaped, differentiated primarily for artistic effect. The heavy, solid "frontispiece" into which the Richardsonian romanesque entry arch is set seems at odds with the columnar openness of the ground floor on either side (figs. 23 and 25). The highly polished columns support heavy rusticated granite lintels, also Richardsonian, yet between the columns are displayed two-story projecting bays of glass in light metal frames.[38]

The exterior is articulated in a vaguely Moorish romanesque, or "Moresque" as a local paper called it. Others said the "decoration [was] suggestive of Arabic motives." An early historian called it "East Indian or Hindoo," describing it as ". . . a wayward child of Root's seething brain, an architectural tour de force." Monroe reported that "Root himself always doubted whether its wealth of ornament would endure the test of time." Peter Brooks said he preferred the "plain massiveness" of Richardson's exteriors. Nevertheless, the fineness of the subtle molding of brick cannot be denied (fig. 24). If today the Rookery's exterior looks overwrought, Root's sensitive and sure handling of materials can still be appreciated.[39]

The Rookery's plan proved more enduring. The hollow square plan was subsequently widely used, by Burnham and Root as well as by others. So powerful was its effect in the Rookery, that Schuyler incorrectly attributed the invention of this type to Burnham and Root:

> If it is not so uniquely impressive now, it is because such a project, when it has once been successfully executed, becomes common property, and may be reproduced and varied until, much more than in purely artistic successes, the spectator is apt to forget the original inventor, and the fact that the arrangement he takes for granted was not always a commonplace but originally an individual invention.[40]

At the Rookery, the configuration may reflect the previous occupation of the site, where an old water tank had stood. A building was constructed around the water tank, which itself was transformed into a library with an iron and glass roof.[41] The architects may have

known of the Pension Building (1882–87) in Washington, D.C., which had a very large interior court at its center.[42] The idea of a light-filled, glass-enclosed interior may show the influence of developments in department store design that originated in Paris.[43] Perhaps it reveals knowledge of George B. Post's New York Produce Exchange (1881–84), both in terms of the large interior trading room at the center of the building and the skeleton structural system that made it possible.[44]

Even if not invented by the firm, the Rookery strategy provided a solution so successful that there seemed an absolute rightness about it; especially in Chicago where the square quarter blocks of the grid permitted the effective use of the plan type. The integration of the ancient plan type with innovative skeletal construction created a satisfying sense of place. The emptiness of the space was filled with the life of the city, but without the dirt and disorder. It brought visitors, not just tenants, to the building to make purchases in the shops. The extravagant disposal of space not strictly functional translated into an economic advantage by making the property commercially desirable. The Rookery quickly became such a desirable location. And in 1888 as the building was being finished, Burnham and Root moved their offices to the southeast corner of the eleventh floor.

To realize just how deceptive is the apparent inevitability of the Rookery plan, one need only look at that of the Rand-McNally Building (1888–90), which was an unhappy manifestation of the type. Like the CB&Q this was a corporate commission, even though the building contained rental floors, and like the Rookery it had a large central light court. However, here the skylight identified not public or circulation space, but the first floor corporate accounting office. Entrances were pushed to the end bays and elevators to the party walls. Perhaps purely functional reasons were the driving forces behind locating a work space in the center, with its awkward divisions and lack of clear sequence. There was no seemingly sublime inevitability to the solution; no elegance, no art in the plan. Here the hollow square seemed a missed opportunity, lacking the careful and ultimately felicitous integration of physical structure, spatial distribution, and social use that characterized the Rookery.[45]

*Fig. 23. Detail
of entrance arch.*

*Fig. 24. Detail
of main facade.*

OPPOSITE
*Fig. 25. Main entrance
on LaSalle Street.*

Society for Savings
Cleveland

*Fig. 26. Southwest
entrance.*

*Fig. 27. Granite columns
of the west facade.*

OPPOSITE
*Fig. 28. West and south
(main) facades. Also
known as Society
National Bank, it is
now part of Key Bank.*

Banks were a building type that benefited from the use of a hollow square strategy, with the large space under a central skylight an ideal location for a public banking room.[46] Burnham and Root's Society for Savings Building (1887–90) is prominently located in downtown Cleveland, facing the northeast quadrant of Public Square[47] (fig. 28). The ten-story building, the tallest in the city when it was built, has a self-supporting exterior wall, five feet thick at the base. Made

of Missouri granite and red sandstone, the exterior is a "very artistic conglomeration of styles," including various Gothic, Romanesque, transitional and Renaissance modes (figs. 26 and 27). The equally hybrid structure had an interior metal frame which supported the floors and permitted the hollow square plan.[48] Surrounding the covered light well were balconies with translucent glass block floors and openwork iron railings. White marble walls also

contributed to conveying as much light as possible from the skylight down through the lightwell, to the stained and leaded glass ceiling of the finely decorated banking room[49] (figs. 29 and 30).

The bank's entrances, like those at Rand-McNally, occupy the end bays, but here vestibules open into the banking room which runs the full width of the building at its midsection (figs. 31 and 32). Between the entrances, and in between the two-story banking room and the main facade, the architects inserted an entresol or mezzanine. At the banking floor level were executive offices, and at the upper level was the board room. By this sectional device, these important rooms were provided with prominent locations in relation to both the banking room as well as to the south-facing exterior on Public Square[50] (figs. 33–36).

Society for Savings
Cleveland

Fig. 31. Mural over the entrance by Walter Crane. A series of murals in the banking room illustrate the parable of "The Goose that Laid the Golden Egg."

OPPOSITE
Fig. 32. West end of banking room.

OVERLEAF
Fig. 33. Board room on the mezzanine between the south facade and the banking room.

Society for Savings
Cleveland

*Fig. 34. East wall
of the board room.*

*Fig. 35. North wall
of the board room.*

OPPOSITE
*Fig. 36. South wall
of the board room.*

Western Reserve Building
Cleveland

Fig. 37. Detail of the original building.

Fig. 38. Later addition in the manner of Burnham.

OPPOSITE
Fig. 39. The arched entrance and bays to the left are the original building (1890–1892). The brick addition to the right almost doubled the size of the building.

During this same time, the firm received two other commissions in Cleveland: the Cleveland Western Reserve Building (1890–1892) (figs. 37–39), and the steel-framed Parmelee, later Cuyahoga, Building on Public Square (1892). This was a typical occurrence in the firm's history. When expanding the practice outside Chicago, Burnham worked to acquire multiple commissions in the new city to make client and site visits more efficient.

Burnham and Root won a national competition for the Board of Trade Building (1886–88) in Kansas City, Missouri. The building committee praised the plan highly for the way it solved the problems of lighting and ventilation, and the profitability of the rental space.[51] At the same time, the firm secured two other Kansas City commissions, the Midland Hotel (1886–88) and American National Bank Building (1886–88). Chicago clients had commissioned the Midland Hotel. It was another transitional hybrid structure of bearing walls and metal frame, with a light well and a skylit court. During construction a truss fell, killing one workman and injuring others. Burnham went to Kansas City, bore the burden, and testified at the coroner's inquest. Burnham wrote to his wife, urging her not to worry about what the newspapers might say:

> There will no doubt be censure, and much trouble before we get through, all of which we will shoulder in a simple, straightford [sic], manly way; so much as in us lies.

The jury found fault with the contractors, but the threat to the reputation and profits of the firm was clear. The firm hired Edward C. Shankland as in-house engineer. A railroad bridge specialist familiar with steel, he took charge of the drafting room and working drawings.[52]

Mills Building
San Francisco

Fig. 40. Exterior perspective. An early example of end bay articulation.

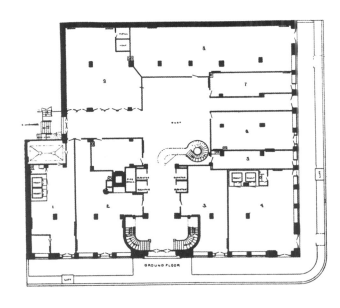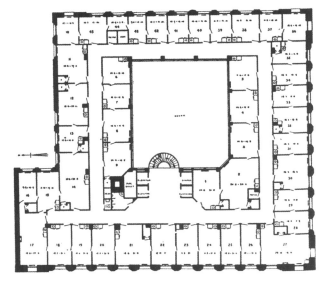

Fig. 41. Ground and fifth floor plans show the use of the hollow square type similar to the Rookery.

At the end of the decade, the firm received three commissions in San Francisco: the San Francisco Chronicle Building (1887–1890), the unexecuted San Francisco Examiner Building (1890–92), and the Mills Building (1890–92) (fig. 40). San Francisco's first all steel frame building, the ten-story Mills Building brought the firm's hollow square strategy to the west: "Built around a large court, and with continuous corridors on each floor, the building represented the latest in efficient office building planning and was a model for later downtown construction" (fig. 41). Notwithstanding the bands of ornamentation, it is simple, almost classical in its overall composition and restraint. Of marble, brick, and terracotta facing, Root was "very well pleased with it."[53]

During these same years in Chicago, the firm received a somewhat unusual commission. The First Regiment Armory (1888–91) called for a ground floor unencumbered by columns. Burnham and Root, working closely with Shankland, solved this problem with huge arched trusses that spanned the 160-foot width of the building. Along the sides, upper floor galleries were suspended from the structure. The top of the trusses supported a skylight over the center of the building, permitting a minimally glazed exterior of simple, severe brownstone and brick. The Armory is one of the buildings Monroe cited as having a close relationship between Burnham's rough sketch and the final design[54] (fig. 42).

The architects were their own clients for the Great Northern Hotel (1890–91), originally called the Chicago Hotel. Burnham, Root, and other business partners built it in anticipation of the coming world's fair. The fourteen-story, steel-framed building was planned as rationally as the firm's office buildings. Its C-shaped plan formed an open light well, permitting the creation of a ground-floor light court at the rear between the wings.[55]

Fig. 42. First Regimental Armory, Chicago. Like the Monadnock Building, a remarkably simple yet powerful structure (demolished).

Fig. 43. Women's Temple, Chicago. The appearance of the building reflects its mixed institutional and commercial occupants (demolished).

The Woman's Temple (1890–92) presented a different kind of problem (fig. 43). The Woman's Christian Temperance Union commissioned the building which had a substantial speculative component. Yet, the institutional nature of the client required expression. Burnham urged Root to deviate from their typical commercial mode to reflect the "higher hopes" that the women had for this "center of Christian prayer and song." Root responded by employing a steeply pitched roof to manifest this identity. The appearance represented more than commerce, but the flattened

H-shape plan of the rental floors was still designed to be revenue-producing.[56]

The Masonic Temple (1890–92) likewise had to represent the Masonic Fraternity (fig. 44). Again, Root used gable-roofed top floors to represent the Fraternity's occupancy in this largely speculative building. The first twenty-story building in Chicago, this steel-framed structure was the tallest in the city, and was something of a city in itself. A version of the hollow square plan, its central atrium extended up through the entire height of the building. The first

Fig. 44. Masonic Temple, Chicago. The continuous facade piers subordinate the spandrels and emphasize the building's height (demolished).

ten floors contained shops, acting as what might be described today as a vertical mall. On these floors, balconies ringed the court overlooking the space, with the stores pushed to the exterior. From eleven through sixteen, double-loaded racetrack corridors served offices that ringed the court as well as those with exterior exposure. The Masonic Lodge occupied the floors above. The roof featured a public garden and the basement a large restaurant. One could conduct business, shop, dine, and promenade all in the same building. Here was the most spectac-

ular display of public space in a Burnham and Root building.[57]

In the speculative office building, the public atrium allowed small tenants to use the grand, well-appointed lobby spaces as their individual vestibules. An urban amenity identified with a building, the atrium was suited to the scale of the city, yet at the same time made the transition to the office door. The building, with its large-scale urban presence and interior ornamental detail, mediated between the huge new metropolis and the individual worker. It pro-

Monadnock Building

Chicago

*Fig. 45. Detail
of east face.*

OPPOSITE
*Fig. 46. East face
and north end.*

vided identity as well, with its presence on the street and its profile from a distance.

Of course, not every building or every site permitted an expansive provision of public space. Burnham and Root's Monadnock Building (1884–92) is located on an unusually long narrow site which precluded a large public atrium (fig. 46). The Brooks brothers and Aldis commissioned the sixteen-story building, which is the most anomalous of all the firm's major works. The Monadnock lacks Root's usual ornamentation. Rather than utilizing the newer technology of the steel skeleton, an interior iron frame is employed to carry floor and roof loads. And the exterior walls are load bearing. The narrow bar building required no light court and offered no significant public space other than a commodious corridor. Two sets of stairs and elevators are located in these corridors, with skylights above their vertical shafts (figs. 47 and 48). The finishes and simple ornamentation were modest evidence of the building's aspirations.[58]

The Monadnock's first designs were overtly Egyptian, but over time, this reference became more abstracted. Rather than applying Egyptian decoration, the whole building looks like a pylon with its battered base and cavetto cornice. The absolutely plain exterior, unlike most of the firm's work, rises unbroken and unornamented from base to cornice. With simple brick, Root sculpts the form of the building, demonstrating his talent in the subtle handling of materials.[59]

The only delineator is the shape of the brick. The ground floor facade is differentiated from that above by a discernible edge of brick, marking the transition from the perpendicular surface to the smooth curve of the battering. The undulating bays of the third through the fifteenth floors are articulated by the shape of the brick: concave molded bricks make the transition from wall to bay, and convex molded bricks wrap the projecting corners. In the bays, windows lie close to the surface, continuing the fluid line (fig. 45). In between bays, sharp-cornered bricks edge the recessed openings; window glazing is pushed back from the surface to reveal the wall's depth. At ground level, in plan, the corner of the building makes a sharp right angle. But as the corner rises, it becomes rounded, until it reaches the top of the building where an arc turns the corner (fig. 50). The shaping of the

Monadnock Building
Chicago

*Fig. 47. Second floor
corridor.*

OPPOSITE
*Fig. 48. Top floor
stairwell.*

Monadnock Building
Chicago

Fig. 49. North entrance granite enframements without ornament.

OPPOSITE
Fig. 50. Detail of northeast corner as it changes from a sharp to a rounded edge.

brick, and the depth of the wall revealed at the openings and in the battering of the base, are the only devices used.

Why the Monadnock is devoid of ornament is a matter of some dispute (fig. 49). Whether the design was an answer to a critique or sketch by Burnham, the response to the clients' demand for the most utilitarian solution, or the result of some dramatic change on Root's part, is open to interpretation.[60] The Monadnock is, however, to take Sullivan's words, "every inch a proud and soaring thing."[61]

By 1890, the firm had gained widespread recognition, having designed and constructed about $40 million in buildings. In their eighteen years of partnership, Burnham and Root constructed more than two hundred projects including houses, barns, offices, club houses, train stations, hotels, libraries, monuments, theaters, warehouses, factories, stores, apartments, mills, and schools, in addition to a sanitorium, armory, skating rink, park casino, observatory, bridge, convent, courthouse and jail, and central mar-

ket.[62] Clients from around the country had commissioned their work; from throughout the midwest (Kansas City, Missouri; Peoria, Illinois; Peru, Indiana; Topeka, Kansas; Cleveland, Ohio; Des Moines, Iowa; Milwaukee, Wisconsin), some from the West Coast (Tacoma, Washington; San Francisco, California), and a few from elsewhere in the country (Atlanta, Georgia; Aberdeen, Mississippi).

Burnham and Root's success in planning and design brought them a national reputation. Burnham's organizational ability enabled the firm to respond to the demand and expand their practice. The firm employed its own engineers and job superintendents, and a drafting staff of twenty-four. Just a few years earlier, however, the drafting room had counted sixty. The introduction of the blueprinting process had reduced the need for draftsman to trace copies of drawings. Tracing may have developed a fineness of touch and a sharpness of eye, but blueprint reproductions were faster, more accurate, and less expensive. Like contemporary business practice, greater efficiency in the architectural office relied increasingly on mechanical intervention. In addition, Burnham and Root now worked more regularly with large general contractors who produced many of the detailed working drawings. This too meant a reduction in the office staff. Finally, some fittings could be ordered out of catalogues as the building process became more industrialized. All this led to highly specialized job descriptions, but the employees were treated well, or as a draftsman recalled, they "were invariably treated like gentlemen." Burnham installed a gymnasium in the office, believing that physical activity sharpened one's wits and contributed to greater efficiency.[63]

By 1890, Burnham and Root had solidified their name in Chicago as a reliable and efficient firm with a long track record of satisfying the needs of business. When the business community joined together to win the honor of hosting the World's Columbian Exposition of 1893, they turned to Burnham and Root for design and planning advice. Burnham's management ability allowed him to reorganize the office so that he and Root could devote their attention to the World's Fair.[64] Whatever prior experience Burnham had had in planning and organization, the World's Fair would demand all his talent, ability, and attention.

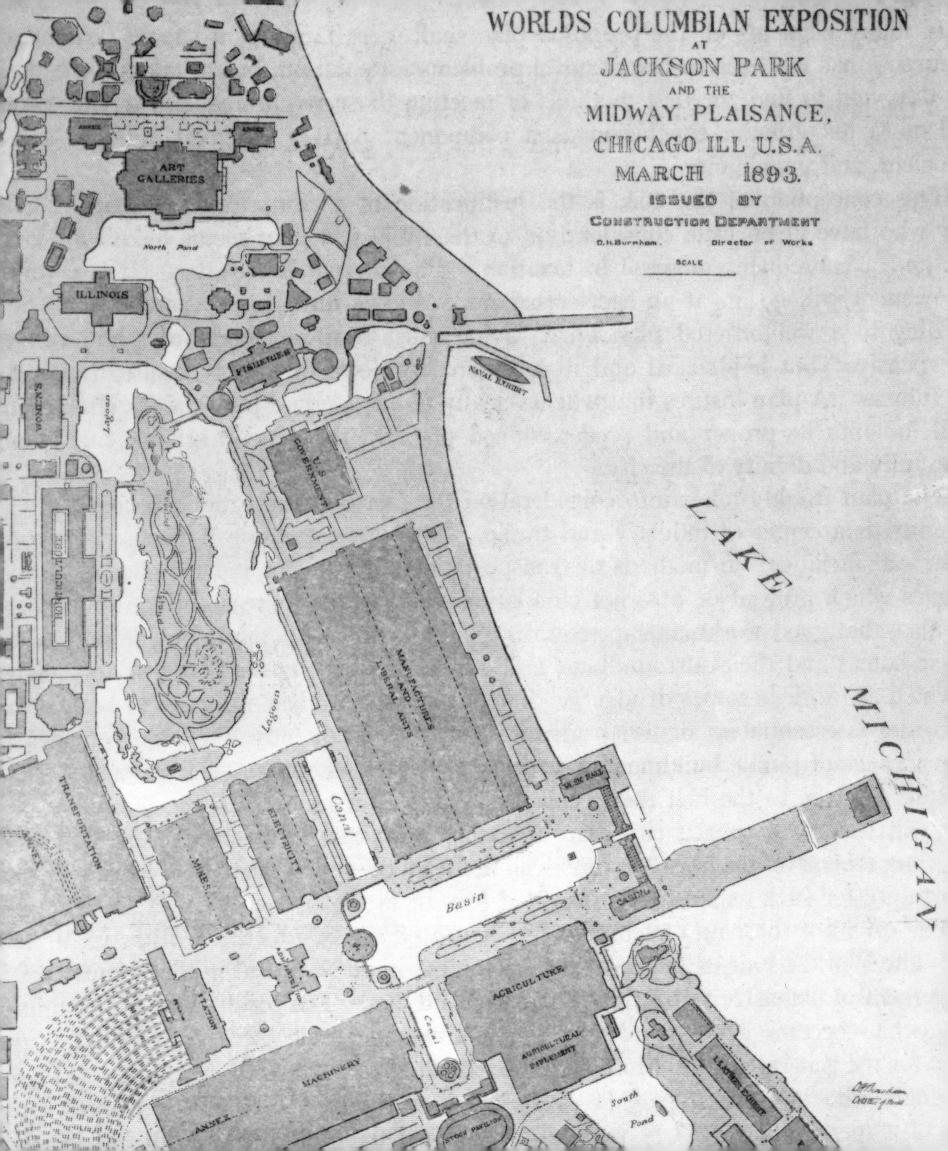

WORLDS COLUMBIAN EXPOSITION
AT
JACKSON PARK
AND THE
MIDWAY PLAISANCE,
CHICAGO ILL U.S.A.
MARCH 1893.
ISSUED BY
CONSTRUCTION DEPARTMENT
D.H.Burnham.   Director of Works

SCALE

ART GALLERIES

ANNEX

ANNEX

North Pond

ILLINOIS

WOMENS

FISHERIES

Lagoon

Lagoon

HORTICULTURE

U.S. GOVERNMENT

NAVAL EXHIBIT

LAKE

MICHIGAN

MANUFACTURES AND LIBERAL ARTS

TRANSPORTATION

ANNEX

MINES

ELECTRICITY

Canal

Lagoon

MUSIC HALL

CASINO

Basin

STATION

MACHINERY

ANNEX

FISHERIES

AGRICULTURE

AGRICULTURAL IMPLEMENT

Canal

LEATHER EXHIBIT

STOCK PAVILION

South Pond

The World's Columbian Exposition and the Shift towards Classicism

The World's Columbian Exposition of 1893 provided Burnham with an extraordinary experience in the organization and administration of a very large, extremely complex problem in a severely limited period of time. The World's Columbian Exposition Corporation, formed by the city's business elite to gain and oversee the Fair, gave Burnham this opportunity along with the authority to proceed expeditiously. So that both Burnham and Root could devote themselves to this endeavor, Burnham reorganized the office, delegating responsibility within the firm.[1]

To advise the Grounds and Buildings Committee, the Corporation hired Frederick Law Olmsted and Company as consulting landscape architect and Abram Gottlieb as consulting engineer, as well as Burnham and Root as consulting architects. This occurred in August and September 1890, although Burnham was unofficially advising the Corporation as early as 1889.[2] E. T. Jeffery, General Manager of the Illinois Central Railroad and chair of the Grounds and Buildings Committee, found fault in this arrangement of equal consultants all reporting directly to the committee. Jeffery restructured the hierarchy. Burnham and Root resigned so that they could be rehired; Root as consulting architect, and Burnham as chief of construction in charge of all the consultants. Burnham said Jeffery "placed everything under my control and fixed so that all others must report to me direct . . .

It was urged by men who knew more about organization than I did at the time, that it was absolutely necessary to have a Chief." Burnham associated a single controlling head with modern business practice, which shaped his attitude toward control in his later planning projects and further influenced the management of his office.[3]

The authority that Jeffery gave Burnham was effective control over everything at the fair except the exhibits. Burnham supervised design, construction, engineering, landscaping, and maintenance. He hired, fired, and fixed the wages of all corporation employees. He managed the police, fire, and sanitation departments. This method of centralized control enabled the fair to open on time despite labor disputes, storm damage, and the unwieldy coordination necessary among so many architects, many of whom were working in other cities. Its success impressed itself on Burnham as a practical and effective means to an end. And the Fair demonstrated to Burnham the great possibility of realizing projects of a large scale.[4]

As already noted, Burnham had a natural ability to lead. Those who knew him said he "had a large-hearted belief in men which impelled them to live up to it, which enabled him to get the best work out of people-a power which achieved great results . . . at the World's Fair." By "preventing differences" he "preserved harmony" among the contributing architects; and

OPPOSITE
Fig. 51. Plan. The railroad station is evident, lower left; the Palace of Fine Arts, labeled art galleries, is top left.

The whole working force of professional men was grouped under departments which worked together in a way that he only could have managed. He preserved discipline and efficiency between them without fear or favor.

Burnham surrounded himself with the best talents, and his skill enabled them to work together, "through his great love of the beautiful, and his power of organization and administration."[5]

Planning the fair began in earnest in the fall of 1890 with all the consultants—Burnham, Root, Olmsted and his assistant Henry Sargent Codman, and Gottlieb—working on it. By most accounts, the plan of the fair was the result of a collaborative effort (fig. 51). The problems of the Jackson Park site were familiar to Olmsted, as he and his partner Calvert Vaux had made a design for the site in 1871. The site was little more than swamp, a condition which demanded that bodies of water be elements of the design. Olmsted and Vaux had proposed that naturalistically designed waterways and lagoons be used to solve the drainage problems, and these were revived in the early designs of the fair grounds.[6]

The topographic limitations of the site determined the location of buildings. The massive exhibition halls (enclosing between 245,000 and 1,328,000 square feet) had to be located on the few existing sandy ridges expanded by retaining walls and fill from excavation. The largest exhibition halls created an aesthetic problem as well, for they certainly could not be picturesquely disposed about the site. Instead, the designers aligned the main halls along two axes in an overall symmetrical arrangement, making a Court of Honor. At the center of the court was a large, cross-axial basin, formally expressed with edges, terraces, and pavements. The designers decided to canalize the water feature, as Olmsted said, to be "in harmony with the buildings to which, in a near perspective view, they would form foregrounds." They distributed lesser exhibition halls around a naturalistic lagoon north of the court.[7]

The formal monumental grandeur of the Court of Honor developed during the planning process, as did the realization of the enormity of the project (fig. 52). With such large buildings in formal arrangement and close proximity, the consultants deemed individualistic displays of architectural style undesirable. They

World's Columbian Exposition
Chicago

OPPOSITE
Fig. 52. Court of Honor looking west. New York architect Richard Morris Hunt's Administration Building occupies the center. McKim, Mead and White's Agriculture Building is near left; Peabody and Stearns' Machinery Hall is directly behind. Near right is George B. Post's Manufactures and Liberal Arts Building.

OPPOSITE
*Fig. 53. Court of Honor
looking east. Atwood's
peristyle permits the
visual connection of the
water in the basin with
that of Lake Michigan,
at the same time it closes
the court and completes
the ensemble of buildings.*

LEFT
*Fig. 54 . Railway
terminal, main entrance.*

discarded the original intention of a "design . . . as little historical and as greatly illustrative of the present status of American architecture as possible." And although Root had been chosen consulting architect, perhaps with the expectation that he would design many of the buildings, they all soon realized that the large size of the project and the short amount of time demanded the participation of numerous architects. Root and Olmsted recommended "that distinguished architects from various parts of the country be invited to design the different buildings." Burnham, seeing the need to get started at once if the Fair were to be finished on time, convinced the Committee to allow the consultants to select the contributing architects directly.[8]

For the Court of Honor, the consultants needed architects with a shared language and planning approach, ones who could work together to produce a harmonious design within the constraints of the formal arrangement. The consultants chose architects who had attended the École des Beaux-Arts in Paris, or who had studied with someone who had. The École taught the classical language of architecture. More than that, Beaux-Arts classicism provided a tradition of articulated public space and strategies for multi-building arrangements, as well as models for processional sequences, and details for transitions and changes in grade. Well developed over time, this was something that recent American commercial architecture could not offer. For buildings outside the court, however, the consultants chose architects who worked in dissimilar styles.[9]

East Coast architects with École des Beaux-Arts connections were the first group solicited. Among them were Richard Morris Hunt, the first American architect to attend the École, and Charles Follen McKim of McKim, Mead and White, both of New York. The group, however, unsure about the honor of being chosen, did not accept immediately. Root sent a sketch of the plan and Burnham had to go to New York to convince them. Before accepting, they met and decided to treat the group of large exhibition halls as a unified architectural ensemble, advocating the use of the classical language and a consistent cor-

World's Columbian Exposition
Chicago

Fig. 55. Fine Arts Building, south facade. It later became the temporary home of the Field Columbian Museum.

nice height (fig. 53). The only Chicago architect chosen for a Court of Honor building was Solon S. Beman. Among Chicago architects chosen for buildings around the irregular lagoon was Louis Sullivan of Adler and Sullivan.[10]

In January 1891, the East Coast architects came to Chicago for a strategy meeting with the consultants, Chicago architects, and businessmen supporters. During that visit Root caught pneumonia and soon died. Burnham was suddenly bereft of business partner, architectural colleague, and dear friend. He was professionally and personally devastated. Professionally, the same organization that had allowed him and Root to devote their time to the Fair now allowed him to carry on without Root. Personally, it was McKim who stepped into the void left by Root. McKim became Burnham's guide, support, and friend. In some ways the two were equals as both were partners in large architectural firms, and they were close in age.

But McKim was more widely traveled and much better educated, having attended the Lawrence Scientific School of Harvard University and the École des Beaux-Arts. During the planning and design of the Fair, McKim would educate Burnham in the classical language of architecture, helping him to see and understand it.

With the aide of the East Coast architects, Burnham found someone to take over Root's responsibilities. In the spring of 1891 Burnham hired Charles B. Atwood as chief designer for the firm, and later appointed him designer-in-chief of the Fair. Atwood brought with him a classical sensibility of academic correctness. At first, Atwood was not assigned any particular Fair building. By the time the Fair opened, he had designed the railroad station, the Court of Honor Peristyle, the Palace of Fine Arts, and other smaller works (figs. 54–56). Overall, Burnham maintained that "More of the actual beauty of the Fair was due to him [Atwood] and his associated work with Codman than to anyone else."[11] The unity of the result, paradoxically, was due to the necessary decision to invite the participation of other architects.

When the Fair opened, the Court of Honor displayed a startlingly complete vision of Beaux-Arts classicism. At the time, there was a general although not consistent assessment of the success of the Fair, and especially the Court of Honor. Architectural critic Montgomery Schuyler remarked:

> [T]he success is first of all a success of unity, a triumph of ensemble. The whole is better than any of its parts and greater than all its parts, and its effect is one and indivisible.

The plan created this unity of effect and the success of the ensemble. It would be a "misappreciation," Schuyler wrote, to "mistake the significance of the architecture." The important element was the plan, which supplied "indications which sensitive architects had no choice but to follow." That is what most agreed upon; the role of the plan and its applicability to the new art and science of city planning. Another contemporary critic observed that it "is easy to see that the plan is the first thing to be considered in the beautification of the city; the other things, the architecture of the buildings and their interior decoration, should spring from the ground plan."[12]

The Court of Honor became popularly known as the "White City," but the architects had not set out to create an idealized city. Instead, they had sought to demonstrate the superior abilities of architects in private practice over those in government service. At this time architects and their professional organization, the American Institute of Architects (AIA), were engaged in a fight for fair and open competitions for government buildings. Their goal was to exhibit a higher quality of civic architecture, as compared to the poor quality of work produced by the office of the Architect of the Treasury. The buildings, particularly those by the East Coast architects, were to provide "an object-lesson to our legislators, teaching them that their responsibilities in respect to our national architecture are not properly discharged by maintain-

Fig. 56. Detail of the reconstructed Fine Arts Building, now the Museum of Science and Industry.

**World's Columbian
Exposition**
Chicago

*Fig.57. Administration
building from the north,
through the streetlike
proportions of the space
between Van Brunt
and Howe's Electricity
Building, left, and
S.S. Beman's Mines and
Mining Building, right.*

ing a costly architectural factory in Washington." The architects proffered examples of good civic buildings. And after the fact, the Fair was interpreted as not only a lesson in architecture, but also an object lesson in city planning[13] (fig. 57).

Contemporary reporters noted that this remarkable demonstration of architectural ensemble seemed to have an effect on the behavior of fair-goers. The "commonplace crowd" was remarked to be "orderly and well-behaved", that is to say, possessing "hitherto uncommon characteristics." Remembering the deportment of the crowd, writer Henry Demarest Lloyd observed: "How little policing people need when they are happy and contented." This was put to the test on Chicago Day at the fair, the twenty-second anniversary of the great Chicago fire (fig. 58). That

was the day "when the largest multitude ever assembled within a space so circumscribed subjected the arrangements for public convenience, comfort and accommodation to the severest test." This crowd of Chicagoans was noted to have shown "restraint and discipline" and no "disorder." That Chicago's immigrant population could "not have been more deferential and observant of the decorum of place and occasion" was deemed a triumph. Credited with elevating the conduct of fair-goers and arousing "their higher consciousness," the Fair was judged to have provided an artistically and morally uplifting environment.[14]

With the success of the Fair, Burnham grew in esteem in the eyes of the local commercial community that had sponsored it. Peter B. Wight explained that "the businessman of Chicago then realized more than ever before that he was the man for big things, and nothing was so large as not to come within the possibility of his accomplishment." At the same time, Burnham moved from regional to national prominence. He had earlier helped form the Western Association of Architects in 1884; in 1893 the members of the AIA elected Burnham their president. And in the years immediately after the Fair, he helped McKim and others raise money for the American Academy in Rome. Burnham was now nationally known "as a man who could accomplish anything he set out to do."[15]

After the fair, Burnham had to re-establish his practice in the midst of a national financial panic. He also had to restructure the firm so he could integrate into the office those who had worked for him on the fair. In the years immediately after Root's death, Burnham had practiced simply as D. H. Burnham. In March 1894, he formed D. H. Burnham & Co., with Atwood, Ernest R. Graham, his assistant chief of construction, and Edward C. Shankland, his chief engineer, all from the Fair. Atwood had control of "all artistic matters", Graham supervised the employees, and Shankland oversaw working drawings, specifications, and superintendence. They had a share in the profits, but Burnham held onto the overall management. Here, in the partnership arrangement, we see Burnham institutionalizing the delegation of tasks, while retaining control over the firm and remaining the single head.[16]

The appearance of the firm's work changed as well. The experience of the Fair had changed Burnham's view of architecture. The fair had "awakened in him the ambition to execute great works, and the love for all that was best and beautiful in architecture and art." Not overnight, but with the lasting reputation and legacy of the Fair, Burnham became convinced of the rightness of classicism. Increasingly, the firm employed the classical language instead of the Richardsonian romanesque and the various ornamental derivatives developed by Root. As Burnham had relied on Root for the artistic development of the facade, he now relied on Atwood. Yet other aspects of the firm's work remained remarkably unchanged. The plan of the tall building in particular, its organization and the emphasis on public space continued uninter-

rupted in its development. Classicism affected the appearance, but the core workings and plan strategies of the tall office building remained the same.[17]

An early example of the change in expression due to the influence of the Fair, the Marshall Field Annex (1892–93) was Atwood's first major work with Burnham. Marshall Field & Company needed more retail space, as the land restrictions and commercial pressures that created need for the tall building were also experienced by the new department store. Over time the Old Annex, as it became known, was just the first phase of the store's major expansion[18] (fig. 59).

The design of the Annex was based on the Italian renaissance palazzo, but here its light-colored granite, brick, and terracotta exterior covered a steel frame. The frame was evident on the ground floor with its large openings for display windows, yet the overall aesthetic, especially in the floors above, emphasized the wall surface as well. This mural quality rendered its classicism not so shockingly different in sensibility from that of the Richardsonian romanesque of the preceding decade, but its steel frame was undeniable. Shortly after the Annex opened, critic Montgomery Schuyler described this construction as "dissembled," saying that it "simulate[d] a structure of masonry and [was] meant to be judged as such." He pointed out that Atwood begged "the whole question of his actual construction," as he differentiated it from "the ostensible construction." Quoting a critic of "Paradise Lost," Schuyler said the Field Annex was "vitiated by 'the conjoint necessity and impossibility' of the required assumption that it is a structure of masonry." He opined that despite "the architectural scholarship it evinces," the Annex was "not a solution of the [tall building] problem but an evasion of it."[19]

It was a delicate and precarious balance on Atwood's part, utilizing the steel frame with classical design principles. Atwood wrapped the continuous frame with a traditional composition of marked center and defined ends, counterpoising the horizontal and vertical elements to create an overall harmonious design. Such design strategies could be employed here because the Annex was not so large, and therefore "the apportionment of the main divisions becomes much less perplexing than in extremely tall buildings." Here at least, Atwood's ability to compose a subtle and seemingly simple facade is closer to that of Richardson, than it is to the undifferentiated repetitions of Sullivan or Root.[20]

The nine-story Annex housed not just the department store. The upper five floors contained "high-class" rental offices around a central light well, the firm's typical office plan strategy. The two different uses do not register on the facade. The top department store floor and the two lower office floors read as part of the building's midsection without differentiation. The location of the light court is revealed with some accuracy on the main facade at least, but overall the facade has little to say about what goes on behind it. What is represented are the cultural and commercial aspirations of the client for the department store in the city. An article at the time the store opened said it was "evident" that the "intention" was for Marshall Field to have "the most beautiful and most convenient structure" for retail use.[21]

So successful was the Annex that Burnham prompted Atwood to develop a similar exterior expression for the firm's first big post-fair commission, the Ellicott Square Building (1894–1896) in Buffalo, New York (fig. 60). Touted as the "[l]argest office building in the world," the local newspaper explained that Burnham is "the most prominent, perhaps, of all the designers and constructors of that modern structure—the office building . . . Mr. Burnham is an acknowledged authority on office buildings, for he has put up more than any other architect in America." The same article proclaimed that "The Rookery is to Chicago what the Ellicott Square Building will be to Buffalo."[22]

The plan type of Ellicott Square is like that of the Rookery, but its interior court is roughly twice the size, and "will have the largest single skylight in the United States" (figs. 70 and 71). Its ferro-vitreous roof covers the space above the second floor balconies, but on sunny days it seems as if the court were a small piazza. The court occupies 70 by 110 feet of the 200 by 240 foot ten-story building which takes up the entire block. Framed in steel, covered by hollow brick fireproofing, and clad in light gray terracotta and brick, Ellicott Square's color palette is similar to

Fig. 59. Marshall Field Annex, Chicago. Historical photograph of the building now known as the Old Annex.

73

Ellicott Square Building
Buffalo

Fig. 60. North and west (main) facades.

Ellicott Square Building
Buffalo

Fig. 61. West
(main) entrance.

*Fig. 62. South and east
facades.*

that of the Marshall Field Annex. Its size however made the design of the facade more difficult[23] (figs. 64 and 65).

The exterior of the Ellicott Square Building displays a combination of Italian and French influences. The original heavy cornice projected dramatically in the Florentine manner, but the entrance enframements with banded columns recall French palaces (figs. 61 and 63). The enframements are obviously representational elements applied to the facade with no illusions of load-bearing properties. Atwood employed them here in place of the oft-used Richardsonian romanesque arch. Previously the motif of choice, the arch could reasonably be used with an exterior of load-bearing masonry, or a facade that approximated one. At the Ellicott Square Building, with the steel frame made obvious by non-loadbearing iron and glass storefronts, the Richardsonian arch had no credibility (fig. 62). To celebrate entry Atwood had to seek a new solution, here using a Tuileries palace frontispiece instead. In the facade above, Atwood resorted to the undifferentiated repetitious rhythm more typical of the "modern" tall building. Although not extreme in height, the breadth of the building proved too unwieldy for traditional facade strategies.[24]

Entry into the Ellicott Square Building begins the public sequence of the atrium plan type, and here again a remarkable amount of the ground floor is given over to public space (fig. 68). The building has two major entrances, axially arranged and symmetrically located on the long sides of the building. From both, the entry sequence is similar to that of the Rookery; a two-story space flanked by stairs to the second floor, then the darker compressed (narrower and lower) space of the elevator lobby, and then expansion into the court (fig. 73). This dramatic spatial expansion takes place laterally, along the longer dimension of the court, but the sightline of the axis continues straight ahead as the main entrance is aligned with the equally large second entrance (fig. 66). At the ends of the court matching stairs spring to the second floor balcony that wraps the atrium. Like Burnham's other interior courts, the materials are appropriate to both reflective requirements as well as to the public importance of the space (fig. 72). The elaborately ornamented open work metal railings and

Ellicott Square Building
Buffalo

OPPOSITE
Fig. 63. Main entrance.

LEFT
Fig. 64. Southeast corner, upper floors.

Fig. 65. Southeast corner, lower floors.

Ellicott Square Building
Buffalo

Fig. 66. Interior perspective of light court or atrium, showing the light and air well above.

Fig. 67. Historical photograph of court with original paving.

stair risers remain the originals although the earlier floor of a light, monochromatic marble mosaic has been replaced[25] (fig. 67).

Newspapers at the time reported that "Ellicott Court" was a "magnet," drawing various people (but not the "tramp element") "to this spacious spot." Capitalists came to consummate business deals in the light-filled space, and office boys to "sneak" a cigarette: "If there is one spot in Buffalo which may be said to hum with activity, it is the court of Ellicott Square." Recognized as a place of "public social and business exchange," the building was "a small city in itself," with 3,500 tenants and employees, and between 13,000 and 15,000 total entering the building daily. In the summer particularly, the Ellicott Square Building itself became a tourist destination, with an estimate of 50,000 visitors each month.[26]

"Not a dark office in the building," Ellicott Square contained approximately 1,500 office rooms in 600 office suites, distributed by a double-loaded race-track corridor (fig. 69). But there was much more to the building than offices, as here again a mixed-use strategy was employed. The ground floor was devoted to numerous small shops, which opened onto the exterior street and the interior court, lending vitality to both. The balcony was developed as a second "prime" floor of specific identity, a banking level for two state banks. Restaurants occupied two locations; a more exclusive one on the first floor, and a larger one in the basement with 400 seats, lit by twelve arc lamps and ventilated by two fans. The basement also housed toilet rooms, bicycle rooms, a Turkish bath, and "other features for the comfort of tenants."[27]

The Ellicott Square Building became identified as the Buffalo headquarters for transportation, with offices for over thirty railroad and steamship companies located there. In addition, the building contained forty stores, twenty counting rooms, two barber shops, and a law library organized for the use of the building's tenants. Doctors, dentists, opticians, attorneys, publishers, real estate agents, civil engineers, capitalists, manufacturers' agents, dressmakers, tailors, watch repairers, insurance agents, and a gold mining company had offices in the building. On the top floor the Ellicott Square businessmen's club provided its members with its own meeting and dining

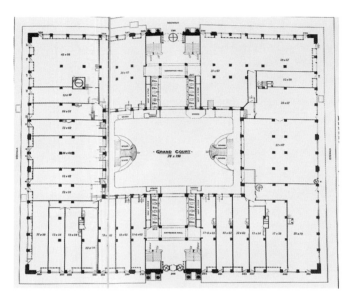

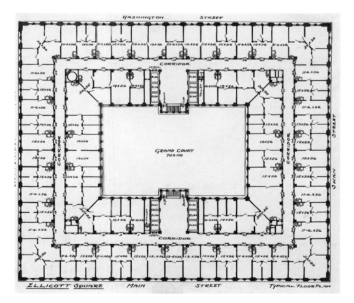

Fig. 68. Ground floor plan.

Fig. 69. Typical floor plan showing continuous corridor.

Ellicott Square Building
Buffalo

Fig. 70. Atrium looking north with added entryway.

OPPOSITE
Fig. 71. Atrium looking south with later floor paving.

room. A roof garden was proposed on the Main Street frontage for entertainment and dining.[28] The Masonic Temple building was as much a precedent for Ellicott Square as the Rookery.

Burnham employed quality finishes appropriate to a first class office building. In addition to the floor of the court, the two main entrance corridors were also marble. The paving of the eight-foot wide public corridors on the upper floor were marble as well, and were lined with marble wainscoting to a height of four and a half feet. Ellicott Square's systems, services, and facilities were of the latest design and advertised with pride. The building had the water pumping capacity for city of 40,000. Its sixteen passenger elevators rose ten floors in twenty seconds; and elevator service was provided twenty-four hours a day, seven days a week, something no other Buffalo building offered. Also advertised were the features of each office: "a marble wash bowl [with hot and cold water], a permanent wardrobe, messenger call boxes, steam radiators and electric lights." Some offices had vaults with steel doors and combination locks.[29]

The building's size, finishes, services, and public space made the Ellicott Square famous. It became known as the building that needed no address when a letter, with only "Ellicott Square" indicating the destination, was delivered to a tenant in the building. As late as 1931, it still proclaimed itself: "Not the tallest nor the shortest, not the newest but the best known office building between New York & Chicago." The public space of the building also permitted unplanned but advantageous uses. For instance, in 1900 tenants formed the Noonday Winter Pedestrians Club to take daily walks within the building. By following the circuits of hallways floor after floor, the walkers traveled 6,273 feet in length, or over a mile. Some form of this ritual continues today, demonstrating the remarkable interactive relationship between the building and its people, even after a century. Good buildings promote these kinds of activities and traditions that keep a building alive.[30]

Of more interest to the eye of the specialist than to use by the general public is a building without an atrium, the Reliance Building (1889–91, 1894) in Chicago (fig. 75). Burnham and Root had begun the Reliance Building for William Ellery Hale, who was a

Ellicott Square Building
Buffalo

OPPOSITE
Fig. 72. North end of atrium.

ABOVE
Fig. 73. Entrance vestibule.

Reliance Building
Chicago

Fig. 74. Elevator lobby stairwell detail.

OPPOSITE
Fig. 75. East and north facades.

shareholder in their Rialto, Rookery, and Insurance Exchange buildings, as well as the Midland Hotel in Kansas City.[31]

Hale wanted to start the building right away because he feared future height restrictions. However, he did not have the authority to demolish the existing building on the site because of unexpired leases on the upper floors. The lower floors were free, so Hale had Burnham and Root design and build new lower floors for a future tall building while the upper floors of the old building were jacked up (figs. 74, 76, and 78). No designs remain of the intended upper portion, but the new foundations and structural system were designed for a fifteen-story building.[32]

The upper floors leases expired in 1894. By this time Root was dead. Atwood designed the rest of the fifteen-story building, with Shankland as the structural engineer (fig. 77). The steel frame elicited wonder when the top ten stories were erected in fifteen days. The frame was sheathed with a white enameled terracotta skin (again with the hope that it would rinse itself clean in the rain). Inspired perhaps by Holabird

and Roche's Tacoma Building (1886–89), Atwood took the Rookery light court facade of window and spandrel bands and wrapped it around the Monadnock form. With its alternating bays and flat surfaces, the Reliance facade can also be read as a development of the firm's own work; from the Monadnock, where the windows are voids in the wall surface, through the Great Northern as the spandrel begins to suggest itself, then to the Ashland Block where the spandrel emerges, to the Reliance facade of spandrel and window, and no continuous vertical wall surface.[33]

Contrasted with Root's dark, red granite facing of the lower stories, Atwood's white terracotta reflects the new, lighter sensibility of the fair. His detailing of the terracotta make evident its non-loadbearing role. The "Chicago windows" were set almost flush with the terracotta spandrels, giving the appearance of a positive pressure within. The lightness and airiness, and the clarity with which the exterior hung from the frame, offered a startling contrast to the traditional wall recalled in the Marshall Field Annex just a block away. That the classically biased Atwood could also work in this mode says much about his talents and flexibility as a designer. It disturbed Schuyler, however.[34]

Schuyler saw the Reliance Building as an example of the tall building where "the skeleton is undraped," and no effort has been "made to 'do something' with it:"

> Wherever the steel cage is confessed throughout, the effect is not different in kind, nor very much in degree, from the effect of the skeleton itself, which nobody can succeed in admiring, although it is true that the articulation of the skeleton has never been regarded as an architectural but only as a mechanical problem, aesthetic consideration having been devoted only to its envelope.

He thought the terracotta of the envelope "a very eligible material in the atmosphere of Chicago," but that it was so frankly used "throughout" that it seemed to him almost an "abandonment of architecture, as much as the omission of an attempt to 'do something' with the cage." And that the covering would prohibit the patina of age pretty much disqualified it from becoming a civic monument. Compared to the Marshall Field Annex, the covering "does not in the least simulate a structure nor dissemble the real structure." Rather than an evasion of the tall building problem, Schuyler found this to be "a statement of the problem" but not "a solution of it":

Reliance Building
Chicago

*Fig. 76. Elevator lobby
looking west.*

*Fig. 77. Upper floor
with interior glazing.*

OPPOSITE
*Fig. 78. Elevator
lobby looking east.*

Fisher Building
Chicago

OPPOSITE
Fig. 79. East facade with northern addition.

Fig. 80. Fisher Building. South facade.

But . . . if this is the most and the best that can be done with the sky-scraper, the sky-scraper is architecturally intractable; and that is a confession one is loth to make about any system of construction that is mechanically sound.

Atwood did not completely abandon all historic architectural references in the Reliance Building. The spandrels and mullions are ornamented in the gothic mode, as are those of Atwood's Fisher Building (1895–96) which partakes of a modicum of gothic verticality as well[35] (figs. 79 and 80).

Perhaps more significant than the Fair's impact on the artistic expression of the tall building was the interest it awakened in the public spaces of a city. The Fair prompted designers and city officials to offer proposals for the improvement of Chicago's lakefront. The lakefront park was a narrow strip of land between Michigan Avenue and Lake Michigan, directly east of the city's business center (fig. 81). Traversed north to south by the tracks of the Illinois Central Railroad, the site was subject to years of disputes

over the ownership of the riparian rights and the possibility for expansion. In the early 1890s, the U. S. Supreme Court ruled that the railroad had no claim to development rights. At the same time, the builders of the Sanitary and Ship Canal offered excavation material to the city, free-of-charge, as fill to expand the park beyond the railroad right-of-way. These developments in conjunction with the Fair triggered renewed and vigorous interest in the lakefront.[36]

Lakefront
Chicago

Fig. 81. The green respite of Grant Park.

Burnham began thinking about the lakefront site shortly after the fair closed in fall of 1893. He worked with Atwood on preliminary designs and in May 1894 wrote to Olmsted to ask if he would act as a consultant. During this same time the Chicago City Council publicly deliberated over the development of a lakefront park. City aldermen introduced legislation and presented development schemes for the site. The Municipal Improvement League, the Chicago Architectural Club, and individuals presented their design ideas as well. Both elected officials and private citizen groups actively debated the lakefront issue.[37]

The Commercial Club of Chicago was the most prominent group to take an interest in the lakefront park. Many of Chicago's business, social, and philanthropic elite belonged to the Club, including Marshall Field, Philip D. Armour, Lyman Gage, Franklin MacVeagh, George Pullman, R. S. McCormick, and C.H. McCormick. In December 1894, the Commercial Club held a dinner meeting to discuss "What Shall Be Done with the Lake-Front?" Burnham, although not yet a Club member, was an invited guest. Among the sentiments expressed that evening were those by the chair:

> The Lake-Front in its present condition is a positive disgrace to the City of Chicago. There is not a back yard on the most obscure street in Chicago that is not more presentable to strangers when they come here than our boasted Lake-Front.

Another was convinced that "the Lake-Front would not be required for docks and wharves and that the change to a park and boulevard system was feasible and desirable." He believed that such a plan "was worthy of the best efforts of the Commercial Club for years to come." Although he respected the railroad's legitimate rights to the waterfront, he thought the railroad could be accommodated in another way, so as to give "the people free access to the health-giving

The Late Architectural Works and City Plans

Burnham's later architectural work relates directly to his planning activities and his vision of the city, all of which were shaped by the 1893 World's Columbian Exposition, Charles F. McKim and his first European trip. Public response to the Fair had demonstrated to him the moral and educational value of beauty to society. His trip and his conversations with McKim reinforced this understanding of the lasting quality, the continued force and effect, of such beauty in history over time. He also learned of urban and architectural beauty's commercial promise. Beauty drew tourists; it attracted people and their money.

Burnham's recent experiences caused him to look at Chicago with new eyes and to reassess his own work as well. He questioned the individualism of his earlier practice, seeing the benefits of a shared aesthetic sensibility and large scale coordination. Burnham also regretted, but only temporarily, his particular contribution to building Chicago:

> We have skyscrapers enough, the Lord knows and may he forgive me my part in this ugliness! Now we want beauty and we want great beauty.

This repudiation of past work and the desire for a very different future underscores Burnham's transformation. His new knowledge suggested a specific solution to the problem of Chicago's appearance: "We have money and we have dirty air and streets, and dirty air and streets we shall continue to have until a great and noble object of beauty is built on the Lake Front." Such an object of beauty would create "great pride," at the same time fostering a "sense of shame" in the present condition of the city. Given a noble example, Burnham was sure the city would respond.[1]

Upon his return from his first trip abroad, Burnham focused his energy on making Chicago beautiful, both its buildings and its public spaces. His former employer Peter B. Wight reported that Burnham loved Chicago and wanted to make it "greater and more beautiful, so that all the world might come to admire it." For Burnham, this was no exaggeration. If all the world could admire and want to visit Paris, why not Chicago? Burnham saw Chicago as the "Paris" of the future. This goal had commercial value as well, for "beauty was an asset that the city should cultivate for its own interest."[2]

Burnham devoted his efforts to improving the lakefront with renewed enthusiasm and on a larger scale. He made the rounds with his beautification speeches, as he called them, to private dinners, club lecterns, and public gatherings. He sent a drawing "showing a parkway and lagoon from the city down to Jackson Park" to the Commercial Club, in an effort to inspire renewed interest in the project. In October 1896, James Ellsworth, a Commercial Club member, arranged a small dinner party with some of Chicago's

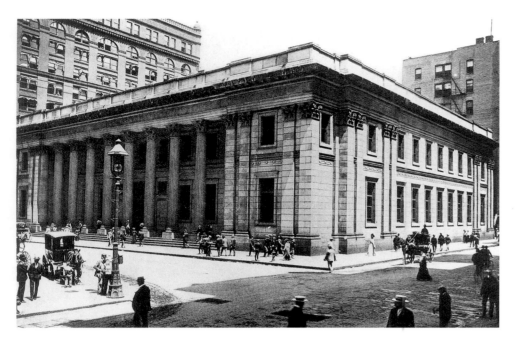

Illinois Trust and Savings Bank
Chicago

Fig. 83. Historical photograph of southwest corner with the Rookery on the left (demolished).

most influential citizens, so that Burnham could present his ideas directly to the city's elite.[3]

The Chicago Tribune reported the event, printing Burnham's descriptive outline and arguments in favor of the project, as well as two drawings. The article described Burnham's proposal as being "on an immeasurably more extensive scale than has hitherto been suggested." It now included designs for Jackson Park (the site of the Fair) as well as the downtown lakefront park and, linking the two, a lakeshore park, parkway and lagoon. Burnham argued that such an improvement would benefit the entire community. It would promote both commercial prosperity and cultural betterment. Although nothing came of the project immediately, Burnham continued to voice these beliefs throughout his planning career, especially in his later plan for the entire city of Chicago.[4]

Despite his one anguished cry of regret, Burnham returned to the skyscraper with renewed intensity. He was determined to make the tall office building an ornament to the city; not just an isolated structure but an integrated part of a larger commitment to urban beauty. Although time demands sometimes required Burnham to choose between personal involvement in planning or architecture projects at any given moment, it is artificial to separate them. The strategies, principles, motivations, ideals, and preferences in his post-Fair buildings were consistent with those of his planning work. At the same time Burnham was

working to improve cities, he was still designing buildings, laying them out, making them work, and making them pay. Function and economics continued to be part of the practice, but now beauty superseded originality as the desired result.

Burnham returned his attention to his architectural practice; making adjustments following Atwood's death and again after Shankland's resignation. By 1900 Graham was Burnham's only partner. Graham provided management stability for the firm, which allowed Burnham to pursue more planning projects when opportunities arose.[5] During this same time, Burnham oversaw the transition of the firm toward an increasing classical sensibility.

The Illinois Trust and Savings Bank (1896-97), a project from this transitional period, shows the dramatic change (fig. 83). Located directly south of the Rookery and built less than a decade later, the Illinois Trust was a serene, classical building of light colored granite, with a giant Corinthian order, a substantial cornice, and an attic parapet. The bank read as a pavilion but of monumental proportions "and, though . . . overtopped by surrounding skyscrapers, its classic lines prevent it from being dwarfed in comparison." Its two stories were tall, roughly the equivalent of a four-story building, and the elements were large scale. The visitor entered through a colonnade of freestanding Corinthian columns thirty-six feet tall that extended one hundred feet, almost the length of the building. End pavilions buttressed the colonnade, and similar pavilions terminated the side elevation as well; but these pavilions were not coterminous at the corner. Staggered, they created a re-entrant corner on the side street flank, revealing the depth of the entry portico and giving contextual bias to the entry facade.[6]

Almost square in plan, the Illinois Trust featured an interior atrium that resembled the cortile of a palazzo. Two stories of loggia-like corridors surrounded the large skylit space. Trabeated below and arcuated above, the corridors gave access to administrative offices. The bank work area occupied the center of the space, separated by screens of bronze and marble from public lobbies that wrapped it on three sides. McKim called the Illinois Trust a "masterpiece," and the design "magnificent," adding that it was "hard to conceive of such a simple and beautiful structure, with so much repose, in so horrible a climate, and in the midst of such hellish surroundings!" He told Burnham that "as an echo of the work of '93 it will remain a monument long after you are gone." Unfortunately, McKim was wrong. This small gem of a building was demolished early in the 1920s to make way for a tall bank building designed by Burnham's successor firm.[7]

The maturation of Burnham's planning sensibility depended to a significant degree on McKim and their continued professional relationship. Burnham worked again with McKim, and with Frederick Law Olmsted, Jr., on the McMillan Senate Park Commission for the Improvement of Washington, D.C. (1901–02). Early in 1901, the Senate Committee on the District of the Columbia formed the commission and charged it with restoring Pierre-Charles L'Enfant's 1790 plan to its intended grandeur. In addition,

the committee instructed the designers to modernize the plan by considering the city's public spaces as part of a larger park system:

> The object of the present investigation is to prepare for the city of Washington such a plan as shall enable future development along the lines originally planned—namely, the treatment of the city as a work of civic art—and to develop the outlying parks as portions of a single well-considered system.

The Washington plan was an ideal project for Burnham. It reprised the team strategy of the Fair, including some of the same players. It entailed designing an urban ensemble and creating a supporting landscape of both formal and naturalistic design, as well as planning on a large scale. The project also required research into historical precedents.[8]

The commission, seeking to better understand the original plan and influences on L'Enfant, George

Fig. 84. Washington, D.C. Park system plan proposed by the Senate Park Commission.

Fig. 85. Washington, D.C. Senate Park Commission's proposed treatment of Washington Monument grounds and the Mall. The commission called for the restoration of formal axes from the Capitol to the Washington Monument, and then beyond to a proposed Lincoln Memorial; and from the White House to the Monument, and then beyond to what is now the site of the Jefferson Memorial.

Penn Station
Pittsburgh

OPPOSITE
Fig. 86. Entry facade with the rotunda. Also called Union Station.

OVERLEAF
Fig. 87. The rotunda is a dramatic porte-cochere that provides covered entry and announces the train station, otherwise hidden in the tall office building.

Washington, and Thomas Jefferson, traveled throughout tidewater Virginia to familiarize themselves with eighteenth-century towns and plantations. Similarly, they journeyed to Europe to study major public spaces, parks, and gardens. Burnham arranged these trips so that the commission members could "see and discuss *together* parks in their relations to public buildings—that is our problem here in Washington and we must have weeks when we are thinking of nothing else." This European trip provided another opportunity for Burnham to learn from McKim. This time they not only looked, but also measured and photographed what they saw.[9]

The commission's findings were first made public in an exhibition mounted at the Corcoran Gallery in January 1902, and then in the official government report. In the field of public relations, McKim taught Burnham another lesson by insisting upon hiring the best artists and modelmakers in the country to work on the presentation. The exhibition displayed beautifully rendered perspectives as well as "before" and "after" models of the Mall, which made the proposed improvement immediately apparent. The 171-page report, *The Improvement of the Park System of the District of Columbia*, contained over one hundred black and white reproductions of drawings, photographs and models.[10]

The commission recommended the creation of an organized park system, including new and existing park sites with appropriate connections between them;

the expansion of the park system outside the District; and the reclamation of land from the Potomac and Anacostia Rivers (fig. 84). Photographs of existing sites in the District of Columbia, and of parks in Boston and Hartford showing children actively engaged in play, illustrated this section of the report. These more intimate photographs provided a counterpoint to the more monumental plans for the Mall.

The commission's plan for the Mall re-established L'Enfant's intent, reasserting his axial relationships between the White House, Washington Monument, and Capitol; then expanded the axes westward and southward (fig. 85). The design returned to original principles, with appropriate formal landscape treatment and classical buildings of harmonious language, mass, and siting (fig. 82). The Mall needed restoration, as L'Enfant's plan had been severely compromised. For instance, Congress had permitted the construction of a railroad station and train shed on the Mall at the foot of Capitol Hill. The commission plan required the relocation of the Baltimore and Ohio Railroad tracks and facilities.[11]

The Pennsylvania Railroad had recently acquired the Baltimore and Ohio. At Burnham's urging, Alexander Cassatt, president of the Pennsylvania Railroad, agreed to remove the tracks from the Mall and to consolidate the lines into a new Union Station as specified in the commission plan. Burnham was already working for Cassatt, having designed the Pennsylvania Station in Pittsburgh (1898–1903), and since 1900,

Penn Station

Pittsburgh

Fig. 88. Rotunda pier, where terracotta and stone interweave the horizontal and vertical lines.

Fig. 89. Spandrel decoration with the earlier spelling of the city's name.

Fig. 90. Rotunda. Side archways with repetitive profiles create layers of space, making this entrance seem more elaborate, larger, and grander than it is.

had been advising him on a Pennsylvania station for the capital (figs. 86–91). Once the rail lines were consolidated, the job to design Washington, D.C.'s Union Station (1903–1907) was Burnham's[12] (fig. 92).

Pierce Anderson assisted Burnham in the design. Anderson had come to work for Burnham when he returned from the École des Beaux-Arts in Paris. Anderson's knowledge of classical architecture was useful to Burnham in the design of the station, not far from the Capitol. Union Station's design combines the elements of a Roman bath with the triumphal arch (fig. 93). Perhaps influenced by Charles Atwood's station at the World's Fair, Union Station is the clearer, more compelling building. It is classical without being a copy, representing this new, nineteenth-century building type. Burnham was thrilled that McKim "pronounced" the Washington station design as "[p]erfectly expressing the purpose—saying no one can possibly doubt that it is a railway station."[13]

A monumental building, three parallel transverse spaces dominate the plan of Union Station (fig. 96). The first is the portico-loggia that runs the length of the facade, providing covered entry (figs. 94 and 95). The next is the large, lofty passenger waiting room with its mammoth barrel vault and lateral expansion into subsidiary spaces (figs. 97, 98, 100, and 101). Beyond, a long cross axial concourse connects all the platforms (fig. 99). This series of transverse spaces heightens the experience of movement and arrival. The space parallels the longitudinal axis only when one leaves the concourse, enters the train shed, and walks along the platform in the direction of the train, the track and departure.[14]

Union Station solves the symbolic problem of providing a grand vestibule to the city, at the same time it solves the functional problems of moving large numbers of people to large numbers of trains. It provides a gateway to the nation's capital as well as a formal procession to the trains, with the ritual of transition superseding technical prowess. White Vermont granite discretely dresses the steel and concrete structure. The barrel vaulted passenger waiting room dominates the exterior as Burnham chose to suppress the train shed: "The railway people will I think consent to making the train shed in three parts, thus keeping it down quite low."[15]

The Senate Park Commission's plan determined the site of Union Station, requiring a plaza in front of the building, which Burnham also designed:

I have a scheme for making a deep fore-court of the terrace wall between the court and the Capitol grounds which will subordinate the depot and give it its proper artistic relation to the Capitol.

Displaying Burnham's concern for context and appropriateness, a site plan of the project locates the Capitol at the center of the drawing, showing the station's subordinate status. Burnham saw the whole of the design—the building and its means of construction, the landscaping of the plaza, and the city plan with its reciprocal relations—as interrelated. The station had to be suitable to the new urban context; it must complement but not upstage the Capitol. It required coordination if the beauty and logic of the city plan were to be realized.[16]

Penn Station
Pittsburgh

OPPOSITE
Fig. 91. Exterior at night.

Union Station
Washington, D.C.

Fig. 92. Exterior perspective.

OVERLEAF
Fig. 93 Triumphal arch facade.

Union Station
Washington D.C.

OPPOSITE
Fig. 94. Entrance loggia.

ABOVE
Fig. 95. Entrance loggia detail.

RIGHT
Fig. 96. Plan. In the end bays are porte-cocheres: the west (left) one for the public, the east (right) for state dignitaries.

OVERLEAF
Fig. 97. Waiting room interior.

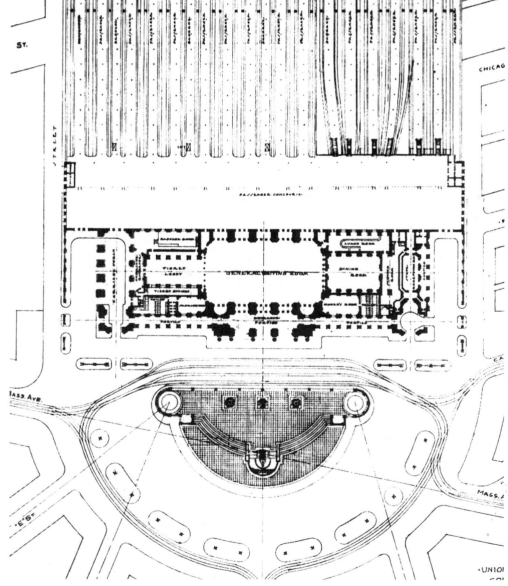

111

Union Station
Washington, D.C.

Fig. 98. Historical photograph of the waiting room and west hall (former ticket lobby).

Fig. 99. Historical photograph of concourse.

OPPOSITE
Fig. 100. Waiting room interior detail.

OVERLEAF
Fig. 101. East Hall (former dining room).

SECOND OVERLEAF
Fig. 102. Union Station Plaza.

U. S. Post Office
Washington, D.C.

Fig. 103. Adjacent to Union Station, the Post Office was completed after Burnham's death.

Located adjacent to Union Station, the Post Office for Washington, D.C. (1911–14) functions as a backdrop building, reinforcing the dominance of the station while providing visual closure and stability to the plaza in front (fig. 103). Anderson suggested siting a Postal Savings Bank on the opposite side of Union Station Plaza to complete the ensemble and finish the urban design of the plaza as an episode, an element, in the context of the larger plan.[17]

The experience of Washington—studying L'Enfant's plan, looking at colonial and European works, and developing a plan for the capital based on classical architecture and Beaux-Arts planning principles derived from the Renaissance—continued Burnham's education. And although his planning work for Washington specified low-rise government buildings, one cannot understand Burnham's subsequent tall office buildings without recognizing this source of his new thinking about buildings in the context of the city. Burnham now guided the firm toward a more decorous rendition of the skyscraper.

The effect is first evident in a New York building that Burnham was working on at the same time as the Washington plan. The Fuller Building (1901–03), built for the George A. Fuller Company, is better known as the Flatiron Building. New Yorkers renamed it after the triangular footprint of the building on its site. Founded in Chicago, the Fuller Company served as general contractor on a number of Burnham buildings. When the Fuller company chose to establish itself in New York, it did so with some Chicago chauvinism. Although Burnham presented a building conservative by his hometown standards, the Chicago connection together with the building's height created some antipathy toward it when first built. A member of the New York Municipal Art Society criticized it as being "an example of the greed of the corporation controlling it and owning it" and "unfit to be in the center of the city."[18]

Flatiron Building
New York

*Fig. 104. Lower floors
of south facade.*

OPPOSITE
*Fig. 105. East facade
from Madison Square
Park.*

The Flatiron Building, at twenty-one stories and just over 300 feet tall, was the tallest building outside the downtown business district.[19] Frederick P. Dinkelberg, the facade designer, clad the steel-framed building in grayish limestone, brick, and terracotta in a classical mode[20] (fig. 105). The tripartite facade composition differentiates the twelve-story "shaft" from the "base" and "capital," making an analogy with the classical column. Frontispieces, similar to those on the Ellicott Square Building, denote entry in the unusually tall base. A heavy cornice tops the equally tall capital, where a loggia-like articulation of upper floors opens up the wall surface, lightening the appearance of the building before its emphatic termination (fig. 104 and 106). The shaft of the Flatiron, despite its surface treatment, is less classical in its handling. Subtly projecting oriels give movement to the midsection, making obvious the thin non-structural sheathing and the steel frame behind it. Many thought the facades looked like screens or stage flats. Despite the good manners of the building, its frame was apparently too evident.[21]

Unlike the preferred New York building type of tower and supporting block, the Flatiron is extruded directly out of the site to spectacular effect. The acute angle of the site, "a stingy piece of the pie," gave the Flatiron a prow-like nose (figs. 107 and 109). The site at the edge of Madison Square, at the conjunction of Fifth Avenue and Broadway, allowed the Flatiron to be seen head-on from a distance, a rare situation in New York. Conspicuous and detached, the void of streets completely surround the building. The combination of these conditions give the building the appearance of sailing northward, drawing the attention of artists and photographers (fig. 108). Interpreting the building as modern and American, Alfred Stieglitz remarked:

> With the trees of Madison Square covered with fresh snow, the Flat Iron impressed me as never before. It appeared to be moving toward me like the bow of a monster ocean steamer—a picture of new America still in the making . . . The Flat Iron is to the United States what the Parthenon was to Greece.

The simplicity and directness of the shape combined with the surface treatment make the Flatiron seem an inevitable response to the site. To see how much artistry went into the choices, and to see how different the solution could have been, one need only look

Flatiron Building
New York

OPPOSITE
Fig. 106. Detail of upper floors showing the recently restored architectural sculpture at the top of the building.

Fig. 107. The prow of the building seen from Broadway and Fifth Avenue.

Flatiron Building
New York

Fig. 108. View from Madison Square Park.

OPPOSITE
Fig. 109. North end of what was originally known as the Fuller Building.

Railway Exchange
Chicago

Fig. 110. East facade on Michigan Avenue from Grant Park. Now known as the Santa Fe Building.

RIGHT
Fig. 111. Michigan Avenue entrance.

OPPOSITE
Fig. 112. Facade from northeast and neighboring Orchestra Hall.

at the New York Times Building by Eidlitz and McKenzie to realize the rightness of the simple yet subtle strategy taken at the Flatiron.[22]

The conservatism of the New York building reveals itself when compared to a contemporary building in Chicago where Dinkelberg was again facade designer.[23] Burnham built the Railway Exchange Building (1903–04) for himself and fellow investors (fig. 112). Now known as the Santa Fe building, it occupies a prestigious site on Michigan Avenue overlooking the lakefront park. Burnham personally superintended construction, and subsequently moved his office to the building's top floor.[24]

The seventeen-story Railway Exchange utilizes the firm's hollow square plan, with a two-story skylit atrium and central light well (figs. 116 and 117). The visitor enters the atrium from the south; on the north elevator banks are arrayed along the sole party wall (figs. 115 and 118). Much in contrast to the lyrical lightness of the original Rookery interior, the Railway Exchange atrium is dressed in white reflective terracotta, dense and overtly classical (figs. 119–122).[25]

The exterior discloses Burnham's preference in facade treatment, as here he is his own client. The Railway Exchange displays a remarkably light, open facade, one that clearly and directly reveals the structural frame (fig. 110). The conspicuous amount of glass and the reflective white terracotta convey more lightness than solidity. The bay windows, shallow and taut, give an undulating effect to the facade (fig. 113). The building meets the ground with clarity and firmness, yet the ground floor shop windows are as wide as they can be within the frame. Ornamented with classical motifs, the facade also recalls Adler and Sullivan's Guaranty Building with its arched entrances and circular cornice windows[26] (figs. 111 and 114).

The Railway Exchange elicited mixed reactions. One architectural critic thought the building might be "a thoroughly sound starting point for the design of a skyscraper," one that was not a "mass of quotations." But:

> The Railway Exchange Building is monstrously ugly, a tremendous affair of windows sashes, an aggregation of bird cages, lacking structural sufficiency as a matter of design in all its parts . . . No! the design is not beautiful—it is merely interesting because it is rational.[27]

Railway Exchange
Chicago

Fig. 113. Southeast corner and the visual effect of projecting bays.

OPPOSITE
Fig. 114. South facade.

Railway Exchange
Chicago

Fig. 115. Main (south) entrance to atrium, looking north.

Fig. 116. First and third floor plans. The upper floors contain both double- and single-depth offices.

OPPOSITE
Fig. 117. Light well above the court, now with another skylight at the top of the well and unglazed openings.

OVERLEAF
Fig. 118. Atrium, looking north.

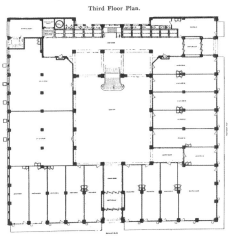

Third Floor Plan.

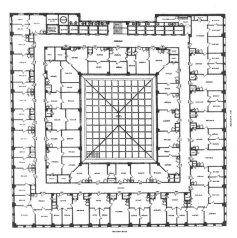

Railway Exchange
Chicago

Fig. 119. Atrium detail.

*Fig. 120. Atrium.
Electric lights are
an integral part of
the decorative program.*

OPPOSITE
*Fig. 121. Atrium
looking northwest.*

OVERLEAF
*Fig. 122. Atrium
looking south.*

Here Burnham readily displayed the engineering innovations of the preceding two decades. At the same time, however, he subtly employed classical tripartite divisions and continued the light palette of the Fair, showing his new respect for the city. The building establishes a new conventionality without employing the more literal historical building forms he reserved for cultural institutions, such as the adjacent Orchestra Hall (1905) (fig. 123). A synthesis of New York and Chicago sensibilities, the Railway Exchange offers the best example of Burnham's intentions for the tall building in the context of his new view of the aesthetic of the city.[28]

The remarkable thinness of the Railway Exchange piers and spandrels becomes more evident when compared with two other roughly contemporary Chicago buildings by the firm: the First National Bank (1902–03) and the Commercial National Bank (1905), now the Edison Building (figs. 124 and 125). Appropriate for banks, both display greater solidity of the wall surface. Both buildings mark a return to a more pronounced tripartite division of the facade, each topped with a multistory arcuated loggia and supported by a two-part base. The base strategy of the banks attempts a different solution to the problem of two prime floors; a ground floor housing low, street level shops and a tall piano nobile containing grand, top-lit banking rooms below a light well. While accurately representing the interior conditions, the continuous horizontal cornice above the ground floor weakens the exterior composition, denying an adequately substantial base for the building as a whole.

The midsections of the banks present a fine study in contrasts. The windows of First National are evenly distributed across the facade in groups of three which are subsumed into horizontally oriented openings. Commercial Bank's windows are individually articulated, and the center section is differentiated from the end pavilions. In both however, the windows are incised into a defined wall surface. That differs significantly from the Railway Exchange, where identifiable spandrel and mullion elements enframe the windows, clearly distinguishing enclosure from structure.[29]

In these first half dozen years of the twentieth century, Burnham reassessed his career and considered the future. He wrote to his wife: "I really think this

OPPOSITE
Fig. 123. Orchestra Hall, Chicago. Main (east) facade, just north of the Railway Exchange.

Fig. 124. Edison Building, Chicago. South facade. Built as the Commercial National Bank building, its replacement facing panels give the building a mottled appearance. The interior is much altered.

Fig. 125. First National Bank, Chicago. Exterior perspective (demolished).

141

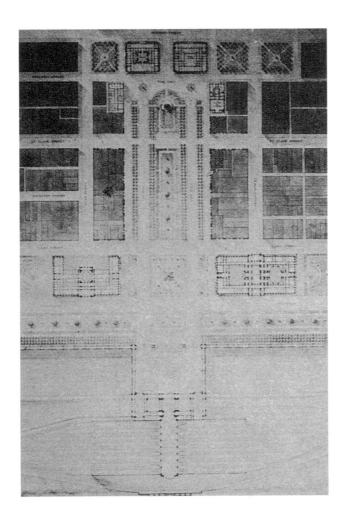

Group Plan
Cleveland

Fig. 126. Civic center as proposed by the Group Plan of Public Buildings. North is at bottom.

OPPOSITE
Fig. 127. Aerial perspective, looking north. Burnham and Root's Society for Savings Bank is the tall building at lower left.

[the Railway Exchange] is my last strenuous fight, and that I shall have earned repose when it is done." After this, he assured her, there will be no more attempt to make money. This investment, along with their bank stock, will yield an income "sufficient to carry on as we have been accustomed to live, and then I can let the younger men take the burden of the day and I can give only enough time to the business to keep it straight, until one of our boys succeeds to it." But this would not be Burnham's last strenuous fight, as he became more and more involved in his city planning and improvement efforts.[30]

In 1902, the Ohio governor appointed John M. Carrère, Arnold W. Brunner, and Burnham (as chair) to the Group Plan Commission for Cleveland. As with the Washington plan, the commission received the support of enlightened government officials, including the city's progressive mayor, Tom L. Johnson. For his work on this, Burnham accepted a fee so as not to embarrass the other members of the plan commission. It was the only compensation he would

accept for his planning work; the rest he did as public service.[31]

The commission presented its report in August 1903. Limited in scope to a new civic center set within the grid of the city, *The Group Plan of the Public Buildings of the City of Cleveland* called for the creation of a large open space. Recalling both the Court of Honor of the Fair and the Mall of the capital, the plan sited the city's most important public buildings around a new exterior room (fig. 126). The arrangement of public buildings included the courthouse, city hall, public library, railroad station, and the federal building housing U.S. customs, district court and post office. The public buildings anchored the mall at its ends, while buildings in between were subject to private development. The commission hoped "that by city ordinance, by public spirit and by general interest in the matter," these buildings would "be developed on coordinate and harmonious lines," although it would have preferred that the city simply acquire the land.[32]

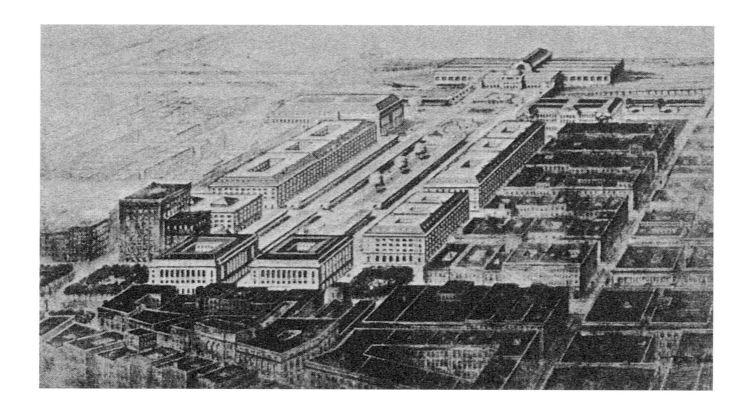

A thin folio of just fifteen pages, the Cleveland report contained explanatory text and diagrams; plans, sections, elevations, and aerial views of the proposed solution; and twenty-two photographs of European parks, streets, places and gardens. The report relied heavily on these photographs to convey the idea of the civic center, holding up the European examples as what is both possible and desirable. The commission's aerial perspective rendering of the project depicted a space lined with low, classically articulated buildings (fig. 127). The federal building at the southwestern corner acted as a hinge between the new mall and the old public square, the site of Burnham and Root's Society for Savings Bank. Closing the mall at the north end, the railroad station site was soon contested as the railroad refused to locate its station in accordance with the plan.

Cleveland was a "real city" experience, unlike the unique federally controlled city of Washington. The small scale of the project made it seem manageable and realizable, especially with the support of the mayor. The federal building, public library, city hall, and county courthouse were built in accordance with the plan, in part because the commission was retained after the initial report to advise on all matters concerning public buildings in Cleveland.[33]

Also in 1902, Burnham employed a young École des Beaux-Arts graduate to work on a United States Military Academy campus plan. Their classical entry did not win the West Point competition, but Burnham was impressed enough by Edward H. Bennett to hire him permanently.[34] Burnham entrusted Bennett with a series of small but meaningful commissions, the design of fieldhouses for the South Park Commission. J. Frank Foster, Superintendent of the South Parks, developed the fieldhouse concept as a vehicle to teach responsible citizenship to the city's underclass, especially recent immigrants, as well as to keep "the boys and girls out of mischief." The fieldhouses contained not only gymnasiums, but also public bathing facilities with towels and soap, a lunch room, a classroom for history lessons and vocational training, a public

Sherman Park
Chicago

Fig. 128. An early example of the neighbor parks done with the Olmsted Brothers.

health dispensary, and a branch of the public library, depending on the size of the site.[35]

The South Park Commission designated fourteen sites, and by 1904 all the design work was done and ten of the parks were nearly complete. The Olmsted Brothers handled the landscape design. Bennett designed the fieldhouses including those at Sherman Park (1904–05), Bessemer Park (1905), and Armour Square (1905), and supervised construction. Burnham himself advised the Commission on small parks plans in general[36] (figs. 128–130).

In 1904, Harvard University appointed Burnham to its Committee on Fine Arts and Architecture on the state of the campus. Co-authored by Burnham, the 1905 committee report noticed with regret the lack of harmony among the campus buildings. Its authors expressed concern about the effect of these "disorderly" surroundings on "the undergraduate mind in its most formative period." Should not the material conditions of the campus be as orderly as the intellectual work it supports and houses? The report observed that "while only certain of the students enter deeply enough into the intellectual life of the univer-

sity to reap the full benefit of its training . . . all of them . . . are subjected to the insistent teaching of material environment." The single "persuasive influence" on all Harvard men, it argued, was "the outward aspect of the University." These sentiments reflect Burnham's philosophy concerning the individual's relationship to the physical environment.[37]

The years 1904 and 1905 were exceptionally busy for Burnham. He worked on two major planning projects at the same time: a plan for San Francisco and plans for Manila and the new city of Baguio in the Philippines. For the first time, Burnham would be solely responsible for the plans, but he relied heavily on Bennett and Anderson. With these projects, the entire city was open to consideration.

In 1904, the Association for the Improvement and Adornment of San Francisco, a citizen's group led by former progressive mayor James D. Phelan, hired Burnham to develop a plan for the city. Burnham went to San Francisco, installed Bennett in a cabin on Twin Peaks overlooking the city, sketched out the main lines of the plan, and then left for the Philippines. Bennett had responsibility for working out the

Fuller Park
Chicago

Fig. 129. One of the last of the firm's fieldhouses.

Fig. 130. Fieldhouse.

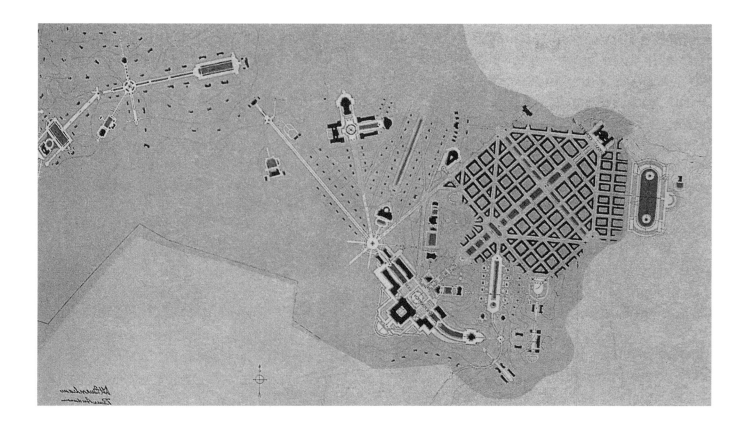

Fig. 131. Baguio,
Philippines. Plan for
the summer capital.

plan and its details. Burnham returned from the Philippines in spring 1905, commuting for a while between San Francisco and Chicago. Burnham submitted the finished plan to the Association, who in turn officially presented it to the mayor and Board of Supervisors in September 1905. The city printed 3,000 copies of *The Report on a Plan for San Francisco* for public distribution.[38]

The plan for San Francisco differed in its complexity from those for Cleveland or Washington. The report explained that:

> It is proposed to make a comprehensive plan of San Francisco, based upon the present streets, parks and other public places and grounds, which shall interfere as little as possible with the rectangular street system of the city.

In order to give identity to the grid and to improve connections within the city, Burnham recommended the creation of an encircling boulevard and a number of diagonal avenues. He proposed a multi-nodal civic center with city hall improved on its present site, connected by a new diagonal street to a new opera house, which itself was on axis with the new Union station. He urged that the city's hills be taken over for parks, with access roads planned in accordance with topog-

raphy. Burnham's report was limited to the public places of the city and designed to be achieved incrementally.[39]

The Report on a Plan for San Francisco contains 184 pages of text, 54 illustrations, and a brief historical account of the city by Phelan. Unlike previous reports, it contains no images of foreign cities as models for development and the number of illustrations is comparatively small. It does rely on a "Theoretical Diagram of the Plan of Paris" by French planner Eugene Hénard, and includes a statement on the "General Theory of the City," explaining the use of circumferential boulevards and their origin in the "Old World." General recommendations on the adornment of streets, cornice heights of buildings, tree planting, pavements, smoke nuisance and other such topics are included at the end.[40]

The San Francisco plan, although ambitious in its scope, seemed to have a good chance of immediate realization. The earthquake of 18 April 1906 literally cleared the way for the implementation of the plan. Burnham was in Europe when the quake struck, and returned immediately to go to San Francisco to see what could be done. Residents of the city tried to convince him to stay to supervise the city's reconstruction, but Burnham refused, choosing to turn his energies and attention to Chicago. Without Burnham's personal advocacy, the plan remained unrealized as the city was rebuilt on existing property lines and rights of way.[41]

Also in 1904, Secretary of the War Department (and future president) William Howard Taft commissioned Burnham to make a report on the Philippines: to improve Manila to suit the needs of American occupation, to plan for the long term growth of the capital, and to design a new summer capital at Baguio (fig. 131). Burnham chose Anderson to assist him. The two arrived in Manila in December 1904. Burnham delivered his report to the government in typescript, accompanied by only three drawings; two for Manila and one of Baguio.[42]

The Manila plan focused on the development of the waterfront, parks, and parkways "so as to give proper means of recreation to every quarter of the city." Referring to the new playground parks and fieldhouses in Chicago, Burnham discussed the efficacy of parks as a social instrument, believing that the strategy could be transported cross-culturally:

> The value of these wholesome resorts in the center of a densely populated city cannot be over estimated. Experience has shown that they almost entirely eliminate certain classes of crimes and that their general effect is a marked improvement in the moral tone of the neighborhood.

Burnham located nine such parks evenly dispersed around the city of Manila, and sited a new grouping of national buildings. He sought to improve the street system by introducing diagonal avenues, explaining they are necessary for large cities, citing the "unnecessary waste of time" experienced in cities like Chicago that are without them. In this regard he opined that Washington was "the best planned of all modern cities."[43]

Located in a roughly elliptical meadow in the cooler highlands, Baguio is "surrounded on all sides by low hills." Organized around a central axis, the plan located municipal buildings on a low northwest ridge, opposite national buildings on a high southeast plateau. In between on the level floor of the valley, the small business quarter marked the axis with a wide esplanade. Burnham used this obvious formality to give this small town the dignity befitting a capital city.

Not much more can be said about the plan as, in Burnham's words, it "is frankly preliminary in character," due to "the absence of surveys."[44]

The War Department hired Burnham to put the imprint of the United States on the Philippine capitals as well as to provide rational plans. That the United States government thought city planning was important enough to send Burnham half way around the world (in a time before air travel) reaffirmed his belief in its significance. Anderson's Beaux-Arts training, which combined clarity of organization with an artis-

Highland Office Building
Pittsburgh

Fig. 132. Built for Frick (1910–1911), the main facade and side elevation display different facade strategies.

Fig. 133. The rear light court (and another side) uses yet another facade strategy.

Frick Building
Pittsburgh

Fig. 134. Eastern (main) facade. The present ground floor was originally one level below grade before the street was lowered.

Fig. 135. Building Annex, exterior detail.

OPPOSITE
Fig. 136. Southern and eastern facades. The shorter building to the left is the Frick Office Building Annex, now the Allegheny Building.

tic solution, provided Burnham with a historical and theoretical basis for linking convenience and beauty in city planning, as he had in building design. Contemporary critics and later historians frequently misinterpreted the planning efforts of Burnham (and others) as mere beautification. Such characterizations overlook Burnham's Manila railroad plan for the War Department. His own planning experiences pointed to the role of railroads in shaping the fabric and image of the city, in expanding and supporting its economy, and the influence of all this on the city plan. Those who worked with Burnham learned from their planning experiences as well. For instance, in the years after the Senate Park Commission, Burnham continued to advocate for the implementation of the commission's plan unofficially, that is to say from a powerless position. In 1910 President Taft remedied this by establishing the National Fine Arts Commission to oversee the art and architecture of the nation's capital and by making Burnham its first chair.[45]

During these same years at the turn of the century, Burnham expanded the firm's work. In Pittsburgh alone, the firm designed some twenty buildings, and constructed seventeen, between 1898 and 1912. Commissions included a half dozen from the Henry W. Oliver family and three from Henry Clay Frick[46] (figs. 132 and 133).

Frick hired Burnham to design a monumental office building, and chose a location directly opposite H. H. Richardson's exceptional Allegheny County Courthouse. His twenty-one story Frick Office Building (1901–02) (fig. 136), given its size and siting, is something of an affront to the courthouse, but Burnham did his best to show respect by making the Frick building simple and severe but dignified in granite.[47] A contemporary writer described the Frick building as "the most complete, stately and convenient tall office building in the world," and observed:

> The Frick building is not only a place for the transaction of business. While it is intended for such, many doubtless overlook the fact of its sublimity, its simplicity and the place it occupies in American architecture.

When first constructed, the two-story Greek Doric colonnade sat at ground level, judiciously and infrequently embellished with Greek details. Now that the street grade is twelve feet below the original, one

Frick Building
Pittsburgh

Fig. 137. Lobby with LaFarge window "Fortune."

Fig. 138. Entrance lobby. The doors were originally at the level of the lions.

OPPOSITE
Fig. 139. Transverse corridor, looking south.

enters into a lowered first floor, descending into a taller lobby[48] (fig. 134).

The marble lobby with bronze fittings is more elaborately ornamented than the exterior. A patron of the arts, Frick commissioned bronze lions from A. P. Proctor to flank the entrance inside the lobby[49] (fig. 138). Frick also commissioned a stained glass window depicting "Fortune" from John LaFarge, who represented the goddess as "a giddy, disheveled, voluptuous strumpet"[50] (fig. 137). The window lies on axis with the entrance at the intersection of the transverse corridor (fig. 139). Site limitations did not permit the inclusion of an atrium, as found in Burnham's other premier buildings. The first floor lobby is T-shaped with entry at its base. Burnham developed the space with a wide entry lobby and a narrowing of the space at the elevator banks. He used the LaFarge window in place of the absent atrium to provide a sense of destination. The upper floors are E-shaped in plan, the solid side of the "E" comprising the main facade and the open part at the rear providing light courts for the offices.

Burnham controlled the project in typical fashion. He criticized LaFarge's sketches for the window. He wrote to the head of the Smithsonian's zoological gardens, asking permission for Proctor to study the lions, and then criticized Proctor's study models as well. He specified a change in the top member of the cornice from granite to concrete covered with heavy copper to act as a gutter. He acted as arbitrator between Frick and the general contractor, the George A. Fuller Company. He fought with Frick to receive his fee. After the disagreements were settled, Burnham designed the Frick Annex Office Building, now Allegheny Building (1905)[51] (fig. 135).

**McCreery
Department Store
Building**
Pittsburgh

*Fig. 140. Western
and southern facades.
Referred to in some early
documents as the Oliver
Wood Street Building,
it is now known as
300 Sixth Avenue.*

OPPOSITE
*Fig. 141. With the
Oliver Building in the
background, the contrast
between typical retail
and office building
facade strategies is
evident.*

Burnham received his first building commission from Oliver in 1901. In the next decade, Burnham designed a number of buildings for him, including one for his heirs. The first, the Wood Street Building (1902–04), became known as the McCreery Department Store, and is now called the 300 Sixth Avenue Building (fig. 140). The thirteen-story building, covered in cream terracotta, boldly exhibits the frame. Tripartite window openings take up most of the facade. Continuous sills emphasize the horizontal— an articulation typical of department stores.[52]

The Henry W. Oliver Building (1907–10) occupies the east end of the same block. Oliver began the project; after he died his heirs constructed the building as a memorial to him. The three-story base of the twenty-five story office building is clad in granite, the rest of the building in terracotta. Burnham suggested terracotta to Oliver as a way of relating the office building to the Wood Street department store, "making his whole block uniform" (fig. 141). Unable to visualize it, Oliver decided to wait until he saw the Wood Street Building completed. Once terracotta was chosen, Burnham explained the relationship of material to fenestration:

> The Frick design being of granite gave a very broad pier and therefore only two windows. Your design being of terra cotta naturally calls for three windows and will allow more glass than the Frick design.

Burnham advocated three windows per bay, citing the greater flexibility it gave in the division of the rooms behind, but the client chose two.[53]

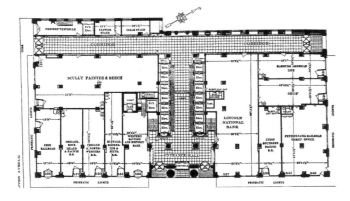

TYPICAL OFFICE FLOOR PLAN—OLIVER BUILDING, PITTSBURGH.

Henry W. Oliver Building
Pittsburgh

Fig. 142. Typical and first floor plans. The T-shaped lobby is similar to that used in the Frick Building. Both buildings have E-shaped upper floor plans, with a continuous main facade and light courts open to the rear.

The Oliver Building shows the mature form of the firm's facade strategy (fig. 144). The granite base relates the building to the street, with its flanking Greek Doric columns announcing the building's entrance, giant pilasters, entablature, incised panels and moldings, and wide window openings for the shops on the ground floor (fig. 143). The repetitive midsection shaft, almost completely devoid of ornament, provides enough wall surface to give visual solidity to the whole. Articulated like pavilions, the end bays contribute additional stability to the composition with wall surfaces of a weighty texture. The building's crown consists of a three-story arcuated "loggia," capped by a cornice that borrows the top floor of windows for a frieze (fig. 145). This, the most elaborately ornamented part of the building, acts as the building's "head" or "face" from a distance, giving it identity at the scale of the city.[54]

Similar to the Frick, the plan of the Oliver Building lobby is T-shaped, with E-shaped upper stories (figs.

Fig. 143. Main entrance.

OPPOSITE
Fig. 144. Eastern (main) facade on Mellon Square.

Henry W. Oliver Building
Pittsburgh

Fig. 145. Cornice detail of rear facade.

RIGHT
Fig. 146. West (rear) facade.

156

Henry W. Oliver Building
Pittsburgh

Fig. 147. Entrance with Grecian details.

OPPOSITE
Fig. 148. Entrance vestibule.

142 and 146). Rather than stairs flanking the entry, a cross axis marking the major ground floor tenants (originally both banks) makes for a more complex space, as do the stair balconies tucked behind the elevator banks (figs. 147 and 148). The lobby narrows between the elevators, then meets the cross axial rear corridor linking the side entrances (figs. 149 and 150). Polished marble floor and walls throughout the main floors reflect light and give a liveliness to the space, as do the bronze window grills and elevator fittings.[55]

The upper office floors offer an excellent example of the amenities and finishes of a first-class office building at the time. Marble covered the floor, as well as the walls to a height of seven feet, with a green Vermont marble base and white marble wainscotting, and glass panels and plaster cornice above. Four marble drinking fountains on each floor provided filtered ice water from two private wells. Each of the fifty offices per floor contained a safe, closet, and wash basin; and featured operable transoms over wood paneled doors, Honduran mahogany woodwork, and hardwood maple floors. Chair rails and baseboards were grooved for the running of electrical wires and telephone lines, and picture moldings were provided so that no holes had to be made in the walls.[56]

The basement contained vaults for the banks; and the sub-basement storerooms and pump and fan rooms. The building provided its own coal-powered steam heat. Since many of the facility's mechanical motors required direct current, the building had its own generators and also sold electricity to others in the immediate neighborhood. Fourteen "traction passenger elevators such as are used in most of the latest type of high office buildings in New York" were powered by electricity. The building required a permanent staff of about one hundred, including elevator operators. Advertised as having the "best type of modern fireproof construction, with a steel frame entirely protected by fireproof materials," The Oliver Building was a direct response to the owner's demand not only a for a building "strictly first class in construction, equipment and finish," but also for "one of the most striking and beautiful buildings in Pittsburgh." With Burnham as architect, one was assured of "a building of the highest character and the most modern, up-to-date equipment."[57]

Between the time the drawings were approved and the first rental brochure was published, an interesting

Henry W. Oliver Building
Pittsburgh

Fig. 149. Transverse corridor looking north. This part of the corridor is lined with windows opening onto a setback light court, which was created to give light and aesthetic "breathing" space to the church immediately behind.

Fig. 150. Elevator lobby.

160

Marshall Field and Co. Department Store
Chicago

Fig. 151. The Marshall Field clock at the corner of State and Washington.

OPPOSITE
Fig. 152. West (main) and south facades. Directly east is the Old Marshall Field Annex.

change in tenant amenities occurred. Typical of other office buildings at the time, the 1907 drawings show all toilet facilities for the building grouped in two locations; the men's toilet room and barber shop occupying the entire south wing of the fourteenth floor, and the women's much smaller toilet room in the north wing on the thirteenth. By 1909, the rental brochure lists as a feature that "[e]ach floor is provided with toilet rooms." The barber shop still existed on fourteen, and now there appeared "a women's rest room on the twelfth floor in [the] charge of a graduate nurse."[58]

Acknowledged as a leader in tall building design, the firm's reputation expanded to the large department store at Burnham's direction. Marshall Field and Company in Chicago was the first of the huge facilities. The firm's earlier work for the store, now called the Old Annex, sits in the southeast corner of the

**Marshall Field and Co.
Department Store**
Chicago

OPPOSITE
Fig. 153. North atrium.

Fig. 154. South atrium.

Marshall Field and Co. Department Store
Chicago

Fig. 155. Ground floor columns are both structural and ornamental.

OPPOSITE
Fig. 156. Walnut Room.

block that the store now occupies. The State Street Store (1902–1907), the western half of the block built in two phases, constitutes the store's main facade; the northern part begun in 1902, the southern in 1907 (figs. 151 and 152). The Marshall Field Store now occupies the entire block. Burnham chose Anderson as designer.[59]

The thirteen-story State Street section, realized as a single, block long facade, displays some monumentality and pretension. As with the contemporary Wood Street (McCreery Store) in Pittsburgh, the architects made no attempt to disguise its frame, but here stone covers the structure. Classical inspiration, overt only in the giant Ionic portico of the main entrance, civilizes the commercial expression of the revealed structural skeleton and Chicago window. Whereas the McCreery store balanced its continuous horizontal sills with verticals delineated by the shape of each individual window opening, the Marshall Field Store subsumes three grouped windows into a single, hori-

zontally oriented opening, balanced by continuous vertical piers. This facade strategy acknowledges the Chicago tradition of frame articulation and window grouping found in the work of local firms, and demonstrates Burnham's recognition of context.[60]

The interior reveals Burnham's preference for dramatic multistory public spaces that create identifiable places within the building. Suitable to the scale of the Loop, a large skylit atrium in the northern section of the State Street building extends the entire height of the store in the northern section of the State Street building (fig. 153). In the southern portion, a five-story atrium rises to a Tiffany glass mosaic dome (fig. 154). Diagonal and sectional views bring a vitality to the interior, an excitement to the shopping experience by making it part of the public drama of "seeing and being seen," and a visual connection to the dynamic ground floor directly off the street (fig. 155). On the seventh-floor, the four-story Walnut Tea room takes on a more sedate character[61] (fig. 156).

ABOVE
*Fig. 157. John
Wanamaker Store,
New York. Historical
photograph.*

ABOVE RIGHT
*Fig. 158. Filene's
Department Store,
Boston. Historical
photograph.*

RIGHT
*Fig. 159. Selfridge
Department Store,
London. Historical
photograph.*

LEFT
Fig. 160. Alms and Doepke Addition, Cincinnati. South facade, with older building to the left.

ABOVE
Fig. 161. Alms and Doepke Addition, Cincinnati. Exterior detail.

BELOW
Fig. 162. May Company, Cleveland. North facade overlooking Public Square.

In this first decade of the twentieth century, Burnham designed department stores for some of the biggest names in retail: Gimbel Brothers (Milwaukee and New York), Wanamaker (New York and Philadelphia) (fig. 157), Selfridge (London) (fig. 159), and the unbuilt Eaton's (Toronto). He also took smaller commissions like those for Alms & Doepke in Cincinnati (figs. 160 and 161) and Charles A. Stevens in Chicago. At the time of his death, Burnham had in the office projects for Filene's Department Store (Boston) (fig. 158) and the May Company (Cleveland) (fig. 162).

The John Wanamaker Store (1902–1911) in Philadelphia, the largest retail building in the world

John Wanamaker Store
Philadelphia

Fig. 163. North facade.

OPPOSITE
Fig. 164. West entrance, across the street from Philadelphia City Hall.

when it was constructed, enclosed almost forty-five acres of space (figs. 163 and 165). Like Marshall Field, the twelve-story Wanamaker store was built in stages and occupied an entire block. Its facade, however, relies on more overtly historical references to the Italian Renaissance. In this older city, the more circumspect facade is less baldly commercial, yet Burnham insisted it expressed "the direct practical requirements of modern merchandizing." Its location adjacent to City Hall offered another impetus for decorum. Not new to working in Philadelphia, Burn-

ham had already proven himself with the Land Title Office Building (1897) and its larger addition (1902)[62] (figs. 167–169).

Clad in Maine granite, the Wanamaker base, midsection, and top are clearly articulated. Tuscan columns replace the ground floor pilasters only at the entrances, although Burnham had hoped to wrap the entire base with sixty-four polished granite columns (fig. 164). The hollow rectangular plan has a five-story skylit Grand Court at the center (fig. 166). Smaller multistory spaces—the Greek and Egyptian Halls and

the Crystal Tea Room—were distributed throughout the building.[63]

Wanamaker himself promoted fire safety, and Burnham of course concurred. Two firewalls run through the shorter dimension of the building, dividing it into three sections. Automatic door closers controlled the openings in the firewalls. Four "heavily walled" "always lighted" fire towers were "accessible from all parts of the building at all times," each with two separate sets of stairs. In addition, fifty-two passenger elevators, sixteen freight elevators, ten dumbwaiters, and four double spiral chutes for merchandise served the store. Powered by an offsite electric plant, a fan system with "air wash" ventilated the building.[64]

The Wanamaker Store dedication was something of a spectacle. The mayor of Philadelphia, Wanamaker, Burnham, and President Taft gave speeches at the ceremony attended by between thirty and forty-thousand people. Burnham arranged a private railroad car to bring his guests from Chicago, mostly important businessmen. In his address, Burnham stated that the destiny of men is controlled by commerce. History might not have given us the names of as many merchants as it has soldiers or princes, but Burnham believed they were as important, "otherwise the organized life of society could not have gone on, for commerce is the heart of every community." Among those whose names are known—Jacques Coeur and Cosimo de Medici, Marshall Field and John Wanamaker—two happened to be his clients. Burnham opined that in the Post-Reformation era, it became clear that "the forces that constantly operate to improve the conditions of society" are those of commerce. What Burnham did not say quite so clearly was that, in the United States, the merchant, not the soldier or the prince, gave the architect a chance to build.[65]

Land Title and Trust Building
Philadelphia

Fig. 167. East (main) and north facades. The shorter building is the first done for the client (1897); the taller is the later addition (1902).

Fig. 168. Typical floor plan.

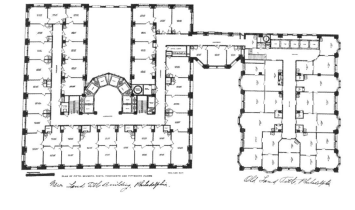

OPPOSITE
Fig. 169. East facades. The newer building (left) constructed just five years after the first one (right) displays the change in the firm's facade preferences during these few critical years.

*Fig. 170. Tristate
Building, Cincinnati.
Upper floors.*

Burnham's hands-on approach to the Wanamaker project repeated that of his other high profile projects with important clients. He spent a great amount of time traveling by train, especially between Chicago and New York with diversions to Philadelphia and Pittsburgh, and less often to Boston and Washington. The firm's smaller or remote projects did not receive this treat-ment once the commission was obtained, although Burnham would frequently make the first sketches. The firm designed a number of buildings in Cincinnati (figs. 170–177) and Indianapolis, and established a remote office in San Francisco with Willis Polk in charge. During the first years of the century, Graham spent weeks at a time in the temporary New York City

Fig. 171. Tristate Building, Cincinnati. Northwest corner from Fountain Square. Formerly the Cincinnati Traction Co. Building (1902–1902). The characteristics of Burnham's more elaborate Chicago buildings are easily read here; the base meets the ground clearly, the midsection is bracketed by end pavilions, and the top is articulated with multistory pilasters.

Fig. 172. Bartlett Building, Cincinnati. South and east facades. The simplest and most framelike of the firm's Cincinnati work. Built for the Union Savings & Trust Co. (1900–1901), it was twice enlarged by Burnham's successor firms.

branch. Then Burnham reorganized the office again, this time to relieve some of his "onerous responsibilities." Pierce Anderson headed planning and design; Edward Probst working drawings, specifications, and engineering; and H. J. White contracts and site superintendence. Graham assumed charge of office operations and supervised the three departments.[66]

Burnham required relief so he could devote himself to his largest city planning endeavor. In 1906, after years of trying, the Merchants Club convinced Burnham to develop a plan for Chicago. No longer limited to the lakefront, Burnham took on the entire city as he considered sites for public places, cultural institutions, and governmental buildings as part of the

Clopay Building
Cincinnati

Fig. 173. North and west
facades. Formerly the
First National Bank
(1903–1904).

Fig. 174. Southwest
corner. Typical of the
time, the west (street)
facade is differentiated
from the side wall condi-
tion of the south end.

OPPOSITE
Fig. 175. West facade
with multistory bays.

Cincinnati Art Museum and Art Academy, Schmidlapp Wing
Cincinnati

Fig. 176. Entrance. Burnham had proposed a Byzantine design to complement the existing Romanesque-style building (1901). The donor, Jacob Schmidlapp, insisted on a Greek revival building (1903–1907). Schmidlapp also commissioned the Bartlett building. A comparison of the two makes the difference in the client's preferences for commercial and cultural projects apparent.

OPPOSITE
Fig. 177. The Schmidlapp Wing in the context of a later addition.

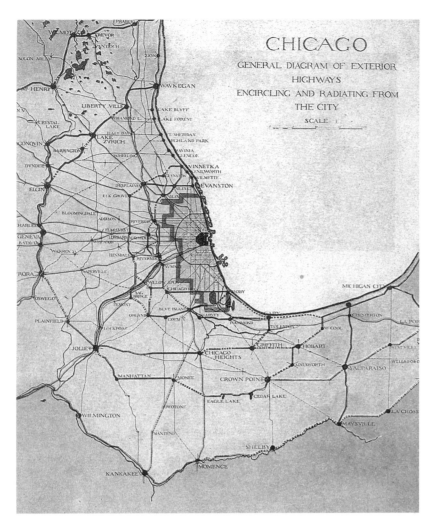

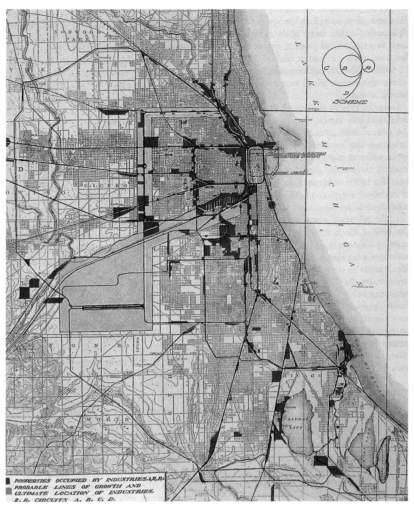

Plan of Chicago

Fig. 178. Diagram of proposed improvements to encircling and radiating highways.

Fig. 179. Diagram of freight rail lines rationalized and related to warehousing and manufacturing.

integrated systems of parks, roadways, and railroads. The businessmen of the Merchants Club formed planning committees and met with Burnham regularly—often weekly and sometimes more—to discuss and approve the work. Burnham drew upon other planning bodies (such as the special park commission), the expertise of railroad engineers, and Bennett's assistance. Working on the plan for three years, Burnham again donated his time as public service. Still, the planning process required substantial funding. When the Merchants Club discovered it lacked the neces-

sary financial resources, it merged with the Commercial Club to ensure the plan's completion.[67]

Completed in 1909, the result was a long-term, large-scale plan for the development of Chicago that included an expanded park and parkway system; the connection and completion of roads in the region around Chicago; the rationalization of the freight handling and transfer system; and a series of interrelated passenger railroad stations with links to the streetcar system (figs. 178 and 179). The plan introduced radial and diagonal avenues, and a series of

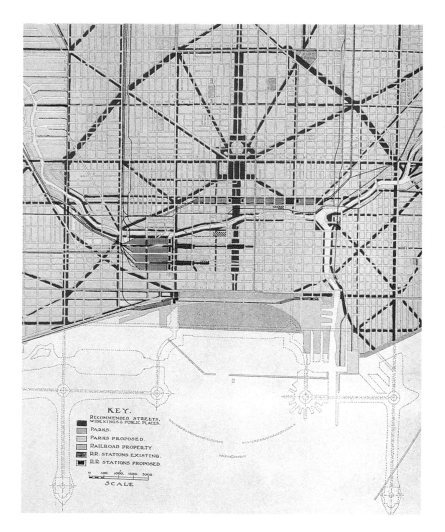

Fig. 180. Plan of
the center or heart
of Chicago showing
proposed additions
to existing grid.

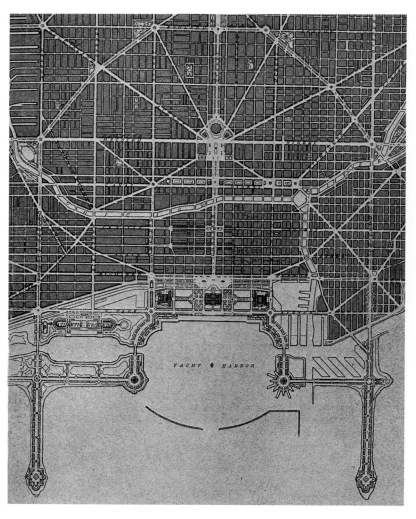

Fig. 181. Plan of the
heart of Chicago show-
ing, as stated in the original caption, "the city as
a complete organism in
which all its functions
are related one to anoth-
er in such a manner that
it will become a unit."

concentric routes to speed traffic in and around the city (fig. 180) It located groupings of public buildings: a civic center for federal, county, and city buildings; and a cultural center on an expanded lakefront park, including a natural history museum, an art museum and a library. Running through the heart of the business district, a major axis linked the two centers. The goal was an efficient, orderly and beautiful city, with all its parts organically related (fig. 181).

Commissioned and funded by a private group, the final document had to be convincing if the city were to implement the plan. The *Plan of Chicago* comprised 124 pages, 142 illustrations, and a thirty-page legal appendix. The plan was well rendered with beautiful perspectives that showed the image of the city proposed by Burnham, not the exact detail. It was successful, and the city formed a commission to implement the plan. Only parts of the plan were achieved, but the *Plan of Chicago* was the official city plan for decades. In terms of its historical legacy, the renderings worked all too well. Later critics argued that the plan ignored practicality and fostered only

Plan of Chicago

Fig. 182. The facade of the city; an elevation showing the heart of the city filled with tall office buildings.

Fig. 183. Section through the city at Congress Street, illustrating the density of the tall office buildings from the Chicago River to Michigan Avenue.

beautification. The renderings, when not compared against key elevations and a section in the plan, have led some to think that Burnham advocated the removal of the skyscraper from Chicago (figs. 182 and 183). Instead, Burnham envisioned a city center consistently filled with atrium-type commercial buildings extruded to approximately 300 feet, the height of his and Root's Masonic Temple Building, the tallest building then in Chicago.[68]

Throughout the plan, Burnham argued that the city is for all, and that the role of the city is to make the best citizens. However, others have criticized the plan as lacking a social program. Indeed, the published plan only minimally addresses social conditions, but Burnham's draft of the text recommends both facilities and services for the city's poor.[69]

After almost thirty-five years of designing speculative and corporate buildings, and running the business operations of his own firm, Burnham understood the city as a commercial organism. He realized that transportation systems had to be rationalized for goods and people to move efficiently through the city. But he also believed in the value of culture, in the need for art and beauty, and he tried to ensure that his buildings and his city plans embodied both.

Burnham's works for cultural and institutional clients are the most overtly historical, in a classical mode, of all the firm's work. Organized in 1894 to house scientific

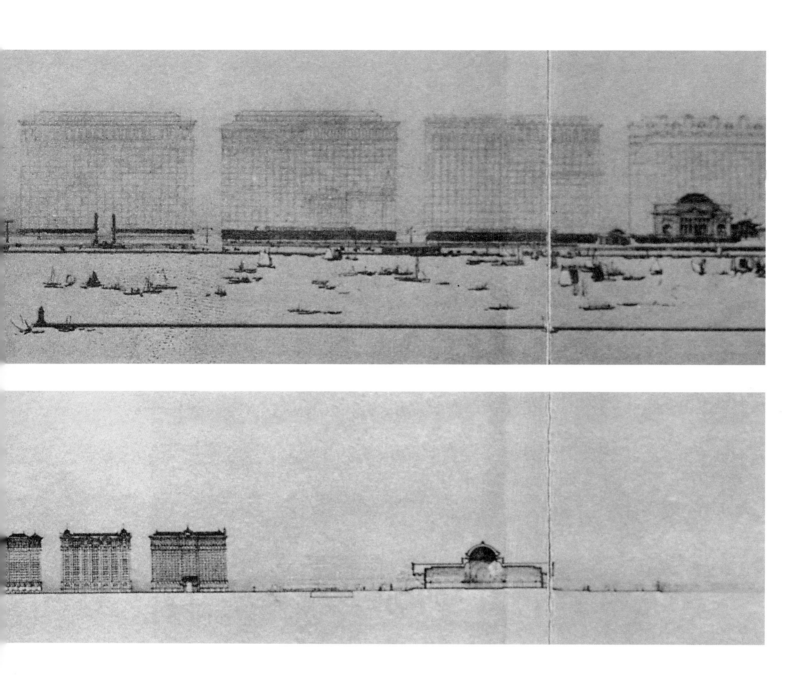

and ethnographic exhibits acquired from the World's Fair, the Field Columbian Museum was originally housed in the Fine Arts Building after the Fair closed. Marshall Field was reluctant to sponsor the museum until a friend convinced him by saying "you can sell dry goods until Hell freezes over" yet not be remembered by your city. So to ensure the legacy of his name, the merchant prince became a more serious philanthropist. As early as the 1895 lakefront plan, Burnham located the Field Museum at the termination of the city's major axis. Schematic designs of the building date from 1904. With the city's acceptance of his Chicago plan, Burnham commenced more detailed work on the Field Museum of Natural History (1909–20).[70]

Burnham's intention for the building is evident in the drawings in the Plan of Chicago, which display the basic design strategy of the museum. Although not situated according to the plan, the Field Museum site did follow the general intention to develop significant cultural institutions in classical buildings on appropriate lakefront locations. As built by the successor firms of Graham, Burnham & Co. and Graham, Anderson, Probst & White, the Field Museum is fundamentally Burnham's project despite lacking his proposed dome. As built, the central hall dominates the exterior. Topped by a skylight and clerestory, the central hall is the organizing and orientation space of the entire building. The Beaux-Arts clarity of plan makes

Butler Brothers Warehouse
Chicago

Fig. 184. Northwest corner.

the huge museum legible. Clad in white marble, free-standing Ionic columns announce the entrances, and engaged columns wrap the building.[71]

In these same years Burnham continued his practice in tall office buildings and warehouses. In Chicago he produced the Mayer Building (1910–11), Goddard Building (1911–12), Otis Elevator Office Building (1912), and Butler Brothers Warehouse (1912–13) (fig. 184). The firm continued working in New York City, designing the Hotel Claridge (1910), 80 Maiden Lane Office Building (1911–12) and the New York Edison Office Building (1912) (figs. 185 and 186). In Washington, D.C., his Southern Office Building (1910) has light wells on the main facade, an unusual feature for the architect[72] (figs. 187 and 188).

Burnham's last buildings in Chicago display a continuation of themes he had begun with Root in the 1870s, but they reveal rich variety in the hollow square plan type, as well as in scale and use. Exteriors show the late phase of Burnham's classical inspiration for the tall building, and represent his thinking, as depicted in the *Plan of Chicago*, that the entire downtown area would be filled with approximately twenty-story buildings. These late works exemplify the size and appearance of the buildings that Burnham thought should eventually occupy every block.

Burnham chose Anderson as designer for the People's Gas, Light and Coke Company Building (1910–11), a corporate commission that included rental office space (fig. 189). The building's customer service lobby and main transaction space occupied most of the ground floor. Colonnades lined this corporate lobby, which was topped by a gabled skylight, creating center in an acentric space biased by the

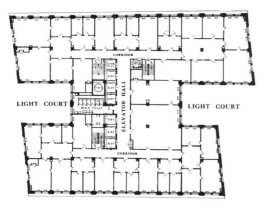

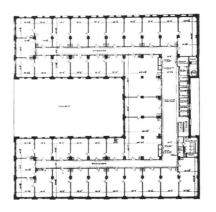

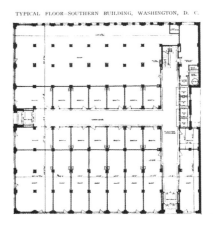

80 Maiden Lane
New York City

Fig. 185. The continuous pier facade strategy was not often used by Burnham on large free-standing structures, but can be found on his smaller infill buildings, like the Silversmith and Stevens Buildings in Chicago.

Fig. 186. Typical floor plan. A plan type not usually favored by Burnham.

Southern Building
Washington, D.C.

Fig. 187. The top two floors are later additions.

Fig. 188. Typical and first floor plans.

People's Gas Building
Chicago

OPPOSITE
Fig. 189. The original name of the building was the People's Gas, Light, and Coke Co. Building. East facade on Michigan Avenue.

Fig. 190. Historical photograph of the corporate lobby.

Fig. 191. Typical and first floor plans.

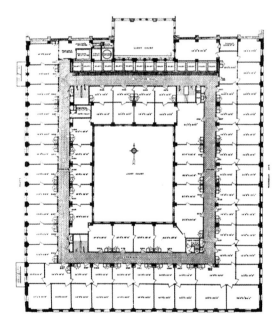

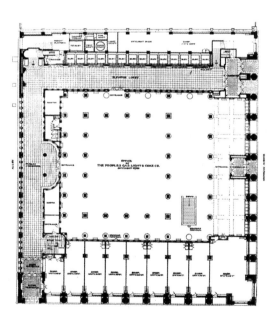

entry sequence from Michigan Avenue (fig. 190). The corporation's occupation of the ground floor, however, caused difficulty in public circulation. It denied interior openings to the south-facing shops and required the provision of a separate public passage. Inserted to connect street entrances in the northeast and southwest corners of the building, an L-shaped corridor gave access to the elevator banks along the north wall. Distributed around the upper floor light well, offices opened off a double-loaded, racetrack corridor[73] (fig. 191).

On the exterior, monolithic granite Ionic columns articulate the base of the building. The steel frame of the building's midsection, clad in a horizontally oriented terracotta, cantilevers over the non-structural columns of the ground floor (fig. 192). The top of the building displays a trabeated, rather than arcuated, "loggia," echoing the colonnade of the base

189

**People's Gas
Building**
Chicago

Fig. 192. Lower floors.

OPPOSITE
Fig. 193. Upper floors.

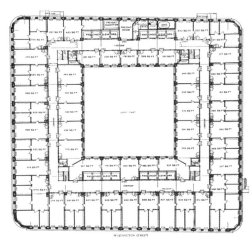

(fig. 193). The substantial top floor zone just below the cornice (now gone), combined with the articulated end pavilions, wraps the structure in an apparently solid case. The Railway Exchange just down the street exhibits none of this (fig. 194). When the two buildings are viewed together, the visual substance of People's Gas is evident, as is the radical statement of the Railway Exchange facade.[74]

When it was built, the Insurance Exchange Building (1911–1912) occupied the equivalent of a quarter block centered on a two-story atrium (fig. 2). Located at the southwest corner of the Loop, light colored terracotta and enameled brick clad the simple, classically detailed exterior. With its ground floor Ionic colonnade, upper colonnaded "loggia," and end pavilions, the Insurance Exchange exemplifies a late form of the compositional strategy, but with uncommon continuous vertical piers in its midsection. Part of the "largest

single real estate deal in the history of Chicago's central business district," it became one of the largest office buildings in the city when expanded to the south and doubled in size by Burnham's successors.[75]

Graham, Burnham & Co. also finished the Conway Building (1912–15), commissioned by the Marshall Field Estate, later called the Chicago Title and Trust Building and now Burnham Center (figs. 195 and 196). With its rounded corners, the exterior of this atrium building bears a resemblance to the Flatiron in New York . The facade, probably designed by Dinkelberg, utilizes the familiar tripartite strategy. Originally topped with a cornice and balustrade, the shaft has a horizontal emphasis in the window openings and a subtle banding every third story.[76]

Of all the late works, most important to Burnham was the Continental and Commercial National Bank (1912–14), later City National Bank and Trust, and

Continental and Commercial National Bank
Chicago

OPPOSITE
Fig. 197. LaSalle Street facade from the southeast.

Fig. 198. Entrance on LaSalle Street.

now 208 South LaSalle Building (fig. 197). He worked on it the year before his death, missing other commitments because, he explained:

> The Continental and Commercial National Bank is about to build; the permit must be taken out on or before September 1st, because at that date the ordinance confining buildings in this city to two hundred feet in height instead of two hundred and sixty feet comes into force. No one else can work out and determine the final plan and elevation and I must stick to it day and night until this is accomplished.

Enthusiastic about the project, Burnham seemed undisturbed that the construction of the bank necessitated the demolition of two of his earlier works with Root: the (old) Insurance Exchange and the Rand-

McNally building. At age sixty-five he realized this was probably his last "monumental job, and I am going to put into this one all I know." Evincing the same determination and assurance he showed as a young man, Burnham hoped "to make it the final word in business buildings in every particular."[77]

Located directly opposite the Rookery, the Continental and Commercial National Bank displays the distance Burnham traveled since Root's death and the use he made of his late-life education, now fully integrated in the design of the tall office building (fig. 201). The Bank's classical language and light granite and terracotta facade contrast with the dark medieval tone of the Rookery. And the considerable difference in size shows at street level in the height and treatment

The Architect
and History

Daniel H. Burnham made history as one of the first large-scale architectural practitioners, building a firm to meet the demands of big business in the late nineteenth-century United States. Burnham developed a modern practice to respond to the emerging technological achievements and economic pressures that shaped the process and form of building itself. These forces created the demand for larger, more complex structures; revenue-producing machines that architects designed, and contractors built to meet client specifications. Architects had to extend their definition of architecture and its practice if they were to compete for the new commissions, fulfill the new requirements, and provide a product of financial satisfaction to the client.

Architecture as a product. It may sound offensive, but the definition of architecture had to expand as buildings became more overt elements in the economic chain. Tall office buildings were more than representations; they became producers of wealth. And with the new emphasis on time as money and the complexity of the projects, architects had to develop designs quickly. Burnham recognized the standardized nature of the undertaking, and the relationship between buildings constructed to serve the new business need and the large-scale organization of the design and construction process. Although sites and clients differed, the basic functioning of tall office buildings was similar, with repetitive floor plates and typical conditions. Burnham employed a basic plan type that gave him a functional starting point. The plan type permitted him to refine and reuse proven strategies over time which were flexible enough to accommodate the particulars of the project at hand. The basic type also gave Burnham a conceptual starting point, one that conveyed a legible aesthetic idea in the plan itself. Not only interested in functional efficiency, Burnham focused on creating a significant work of architecture and not just a banal construction. The strong design concept contained in the plan type contributed to this end.

Burnham favored the hollow rectangle plan when site and functional conditions permitted. He employed both simple versions and ones with sectional variations, and both became common. Burnham also used a version of this plan for large department stores. Characteristic of both his retail and office designs, the large, multi-story space is a consistent thread in Burnham's career from his early days with Root to his last works. His choice of building plan was integrally associated with the light airy atria which gave identity to his buildings while also providing public gathering places.

Burnham's city plan for Chicago related these generous interiors to the exterior spaces of the city. His plan provided new plazas, parks, and promenades as

OPPOSITE
Fig. 202. Railway Exchange, Chicago. Lighting. Both electric lights and classical elements contribute to the decorative program of the atrium.

Fig. 203. Grant Park, Chicago. Buckingham Fountain. Designed by Burnham's successors, the fountain replaces the Field Museum that Burnham had proposed for the site.

the city itself had not supplied enough in the way of such places. Burnham linked the public spaces of the office buildings to his larger system of truly public spaces distributed over the entire city, promoting an aesthetic integration and organic unity to the whole. Burnham showed great awareness of the buildings of the city as part of the larger urban ensemble, where his buildings both contributed to and partook of the life of the city. Burnham defined the city planner as an architect at a different scale, but an architect nevertheless. Just at the time when the real estate speculator was taking over the form of the city, Burnham

stepped in to recapture the city for architecture, that is to say, for beauty as well as utility and economic return.

In making the efficient building a successful work of architecture, Burnham was foremost among those who strove to raise the commercial office structure to a higher category of building.[1] Just as the office of the architect was no longer a pre-industrial workshop or guild, the commercial building was no longer a small shop clearly subordinate to the larger institutions of the city. At roughly the same time the architect gained professional status so did the tall office building. Large numbers of white-collar workers left peripheral factory floor and warehouse offices to become a presence in the city along with bankers and capitalists. Burnham argued for elevating the commercial building in the hierarchy of building types (below public and institutional structures but above warehouses, factories, and other economic machines) with designs and finishes appropriate to the new role, their new importance, number, and size. As major elements constituting the fabric of the city center, commercial buildings began to challenge institutional structures for dominance in the city. Again thinking of the larger whole, Burnham tried to delimit the huge commercial buildings to a subsidiary role, keeping them subordinate to the public buildings of the city. Burnham characterized commercial buildings as definers rather than occupiers of the public space of the city, subservient to the highly figured, highly elaborated governmental and cultural object buildings he envisioned in his city plans.

Burnham's generous provision of space and use of high quality materials reinforced the status ambitions of a building's occupants. His use of classicism contributed to the importance of the occupants and structure as well, with a formal, hierarchically significant language. The idiosyncratic ornament that had characterized the originality-driven early years of practice with Root gave way to a common language. And in the post-Atwood, McKim-influenced era, Burnham took a greater role in the design of facades. Replacing bald individualism with a facade of shared historical references, and by implication beliefs, he used the classical language to represent social and cultural aspirations as well as the political heritage of democracy. Not new or localized, these references were not provincial but consciously international and, as Burnham believed, universal. He practiced architecture as a public art, not as a private or personal act.

Burnham's facades did not valorize function as a substitute for architectural idealism, yet his functional business approach curiously supported his use of a classically based language. Classicism, in its consistency and regularity, could be easily adapted to modern repetition; and like the basic hollow rectangle plan, provided Burnham with typical or standard options well-suited to the design and construction process. It served the needs of the large architectural office by offering an existing, well developed archi-

Fig. 204. Butler Brothers Building, Chicago. West facade.

tectural vocabulary equipped with compositional rules and a recognized aesthetic value, one which responded to the need for standardized mass-producible ornament.[2] Rather than resisting this need with a romantic idea of individualization, Burnham responded with a public and civic language.

Similarly, Burnham developed a series of flexible and adaptable facade strategies that could be reused and developed as the project warranted. Typical of the time, Burnham utilized the tripartite division of the facade as an accepted compositional device. Most of his facades were variations on a few themes con-

Fig. 205. Railway Exchange Building, Chicago. Detail of Michigan Avenue entrance. Terracotta with classical motifs clads the structural steel frame.

architecture was the result of these factors as well as of artistic intent, one that required a leader as much as an artist, and Burnham was both. Burnham was pragmatic about the business of building, idealistic about architecture as an art, and built a firm that responded to both. He had realistic expectations about what could be accomplished yet always aspired to the loftiest goals for architecture. He made office buildings that were revenue-producing and architecturally significant. Burnham combined modernity of architectural practice with traditional forms to create a firm to meet the demands of the late nineteenth and early twentieth century.

All this should have assured Burnham more than a begrudging place in the history of American architecture, but his use of historically based forms disqualified him from recognition or respect as a modern practitioner. The difference between modern practice and modern style is significant, but style is not the only, nor even the best, indicator of adaptation and response to the social, economic, and technological conditions that describe modernity. Burnham was one of the first to function as a modern architect, yet he did not partake of what was later described as "Modern Architecture" or "Modernism." This is not an argument against architectural modernism, but simply a critique of the typical view that stylistic modernism, as proffered, was the only way to design.

Critics and historians of modernist bias most often marginalized Burnham's architectural work after Root's death by describing it as historicist and retardataire. Burnham himself was condemned for having been led astray by Beaux-Arts classicism and abandoning the road to modernism. His later planning work was emphasized over the architectural, as if Burnham could no longer be considered an architect of consequence without Root. The planning work itself, especially that for Chicago, was sometimes positively appraised for its functional and organic approach to the city but decried for the style of architecture which was most often denigratingly, dismissively described as imperialistic. Yet this seems an accurate appellation, well-suited to the United States which has been imperialistic from its very beginnings. And capitalism is, to some extent, naturally imperialistic, requiring new markets if the economic system is to continue to expand.

cerning fenestration and end bay articulation. His facades continued the tradition of the art of the facade as an independent endeavor, not reduced to functionalist expression. Burnham's tall office buildings were combinations of traditional types and facade strategies reworked and reconsidered to solve the problem of building in the modern city.

Burnham established the American architect as a businessman-collaborator who managed his own large firm and understood architecture as part of a larger industrial and economic process. The work of

The modernity created by the new industrial systems called for a new kind of architect. Although often derided as the business partner, as if that precluded architectural sensibility, Burnham was never given proper credit for what he learned in that role. Architecture requires a client for realization, an agent who cannot seriously be considered extraneous to the design process. Burnham was indeed the one who interacted with the firm's clients, but he did not just take them to lunch. Clients had something to teach architects about the needs and functions of the new tall office building, and Burnham learned from them. Burnham came to understand what they wanted and needed, what would sell and what was profitable; and having understood this was able to influence them. Even after the buildings were constructed and occupied, Burnham corresponded with previous clients, inquiring about operating costs so he could plan a better, more effective building. Burnham, truly concerned with function, saw this as one of many architectural problems to be solved. That Burnham's businessmen clients favored classicism, even though they were supposed to be bottom-line functionalists and not "backward-looking" historicists, confounded the modernist who, enamored of technological change, believed that new techniques would "inevitably" lead to new forms.[3]

While dominated by European culture, the United States did not necessarily have the same representational needs. Europe, with its decaying empires, was desperate for the refreshment of new forms. The U.S., on the other hand, was subject to the energetic forces unleashed by new technologies, expanding territory, seemingly limitless stores of natural resources, an extensive rail infrastructure, a mobile social structure, and a rapidly growing population, much of it recently immigrated. Classicism, with the reassurance of culturally familiar forms, provided referents of stability and long-standing values. It was, as in the U.S. Capitol, a symbol of democratic order, not of a lingering oppressive monarchy.

Burnham's legacy suffers in part from the modernist critic's conflicted relationship with modern industrial capitalism. Just beneath the surface of many architectural histories is lurking romanticism. Emphasizing the individual and the unique, romanti-

cism offered intellectuals and artists solace against the shock of industrialization, masking the loss of individuality in a mass society—and modernity's desire for the typical, the standard, against the particular. While espousing to embrace modernity, modernists clung to the romantic ideal, evincing a conservative reaction to social, economic, and technological change. The tall building that gave stature to the architect signaled the end of the romantic artist paradigm. Some of this has to do with the professionalization of architecture. In the struggle to distinguish the architect from the carpenter-builder and engineer, artistic sensibility was used to set the architect apart from the rest of the building industry. Such distinctions are necessary, but in the United States this term was most frequently settled on the facade designer and ornamentalist. One can well admit the increased anxiety when ornament was eliminated from the architect's repertoire.

Architectural history, as an academic discipline, is linked to European art history, whose own internal biases and structures are based on European art forms that resulted from religious, royal, and aristocratic patronage, often from the pre-industrial era. In general, it is difficult to construct a history of American architecture given these European cultural roots of the discipline. This difficulty is greatly exacerbated in the case of the commercially driven speculative skyscraper with its extreme conditions of industrial motivation and capitalistic intent in a democratic society where the client is not necessarily well-ingrained in a hereditary system of power, culture, and influence. The preciousness of art history simply did not fit the broad shoulders of the architectural history of the tall office building in Chicago. Lingering European notions of art patronage, as well as the art community's aversion to commerce, have also shaded the definition of the architect. The so-called modern architect was still circumscribed by older European notions. In addition, Burnham's contribution could not be easily understood as his work did not fit the dominant model of modern style that could be made to relate to painting and sculpture in a survey of art history. Burnham's significance as a modern architect was lost trying to force the big foot of architecture into the glass slipper of art history.[4]

205

AMERICAN BUSINESS CENTER
INTERNATIONAL BUSINESS ASSOCIATES
FULL LINE STAFFING FACILITY

Notes

Preface

1. John Burchard Albert Bush-Brown, *The Architecture of America: A Social and Cultural History* (Little Brown & Company, 1961), 296.
2. Daniel Willis, "In the Shadow of a Giant," *Harvard Design Magazine,* Number 14 (Summer 2001), 38.
3. Harriet Monroe as quoted by Thomas S. Hines, *Burnham of Chicago: Architect and Planner* (The University of Chicago Press, 1979), 22–24.
4. Louis H. Sullivan, *The Autobiography of an Idea* (Dover Publishing, Inc., 1956), 309.
5. Donald Hoffmann, *The Architecture of John Wellborn Root* (Johns Hopkins University Press, 1973), 156–64.
6. Louis H. Sullivan, 286.
7. Frank Lloyd Wright, untitled note, *Architectural Record,* XXXII (August 1912), 184.
8. Louis H. Sullivan, 324.
9. Sigfried Gidion as quoted by James Marston Fitch, *American Building: The Forces That Shape It* (Houghton Mifflin Company, 1948), 124.
10. James Marston Fitch, *American Building: The Forces That Shape It* (Houghton Mifflin Company 1948), 124.
11. Montgomery Schuyler, *American Architecture and Other Writings,* Edited by William H. Jordy and Ralph Coe (Atheneum, 1964), 290–92.
12. Lewis Mumford, *Sticks and Stones: A Study of American Architecture and Civilization* (W.W. Norton and Company, Inc., 1924), 130–31.

Introduction:
The Architect and Chicago

1. Donald L. Miller, *City of the Century: The Epic of Chicago and the Making of America* (New York: Simon & Schuster, 1996) 52–53 & 558, note 45. However, during dry spells the portage could be up to nine miles long. See also William Cronon, *Nature's Metropolis: Chicago and the Great West* (New York: W. W. Norton & Company, 1991).
2. Burnham to Elizabeth Burnham, 11 May 1868, Burnham Papers, Art Institute of Chicago.
3. Louis H. Sullivan, *The Autobiography of an Idea* (New York: Dover Publications, Inc., 1956 [1924]) 285–86, 314. Mary N. Woods, *From Craft to Profession: The Practice of Architecture in Nineteenth-Century America* (Berkeley: University of California Press, 1999) 118–20. Most offices operated as partnerships until the 1970s. Woods, 121. A. N. Rebori, "The Work of Burnham & Root, D. H. Burnham, D. H. Burnham & Co., and Graham, Burnham & Co.," *Architectural Record* XXXVIII (July 1915) 34.
4. Arnold Lewis, *An Early Encounter with Tomorrow: Europeans, Chicago's Loop, and the World's Columbian Exposition* (Urbana: University of Illinois Press, 1997) 58–66.
5. Of course architects did in part function as artists, but also needed to stay in business. See Robert Bruegmann, *The Architects and the City: Holabird & Roche of Chicago, 1880–1918* (Chicago: The University of Chicago Press, 1997) xiii–xiv. Bruegmann's book is essential for anyone interested in the American skyscraper and the practice of architecture in Chicago at the turn of the twentieth century. The East Coast architect quoted was Robert S. Peabody, Woods, 138. See also Woods, 161.
6. Peter B. Wight, "Daniel Hudson Burnham: An Appreciation," *Architectural Record* XXXII (August 1912) 178; hereafter referred to as Wight, 1912. Sullivan's remarks on Burnham contain admiration mixed with a disparaging view of Burnham's architecture. Sullivan, 286. Burnham quoted in Donald Hoffmann, *The Architecture of John Wellborn Root* (Baltimore: The Johns Hopkins University Press, 1973) 88, and in Sullivan, 291.
7. The quotes are by William Holabird and Howard Shaw, from "Daniel Hudson Burnham: An Appreciation," *Architectural Record* XXXII (August 1912) 185. Montgomery Schuyler, "Great American Architects Series: Part II.—D. H. Burnham & Co.," *Architectural Record* (December 1895) 50 & 53.
8. Wight, 1912, 183. Peter B. Wight, "Daniel Hudson Burnham and His Associates," *Architectural Record* XXXVIII (July 1915) 10; hereafter referred to as Wight, 1915; and Charles Moore, *Daniel H. Burnham: Architect, Planner of Cities* (New York: Da Capo Press, 1968 [1921]) I, 83.
9. Rebori, 34; Woods, 140 & 127.
10. Louis H. Sullivan, "The Tall Office Building Artistically Considered" [1896], in *America Builds: Source Documents in American Architecture and Planning*, Leland M. Roth, ed. (New York: Harper & Row, 1983) 341. See Roth's note, 340, for the publication history of this article. Bruegmann, 25: "art was the ornament that was added to construction."
11. Moore, I, 83–84; Rebori, 69; Wight, 1915, 7.
12. "Daniel H. Burnham, Past President, A. I. A.: In Memoriam," *Quarterly Bulletin of the American Institute of Architects* XIII (July 1912) 138. Woods, 125. William E. Parsons, "Burnham as a Pioneer in City Planning," *Architectural Record* XXXVIII (July 1915) 14. Moore, I, 17. Paul Lautrup and Frank Lloyd Wright, "Daniel Hudson Burnham: An Appreciation," *Architectural Record,* XXXII (August 1912) 185 and 184, respectively.
13. William R. Mead, of McKim, Mead and White, affirmed that "While Burnham devoted the last years of his life to City Planning, he was first of all an architect . . . I am sure that he would never have thought it possible to take up City Planning except as an architect." William R. Mead to Charles Moore, 21 March 1918, Charles F. McKim Papers, Library of Congress. My thanks to Mary N. Woods for providing me with a copy of this quote. Charles Moore, who worked with Burnham on plans for both Washington, D.C., and Chicago, agreed with this "idea that a man should be an architect first and a city planner afterward," and he was "quite sure" that Burnham "felt this very keenly." Charles Moore to Daniel Burnham, Jr., 23 March 1918, Burnham Papers, Art Institute of Chicago.
14. Burnham to Elizabeth Burnham, 24 November 1867, and 1 December 1867, Burnham Papers, Art Institute of Chicago. Frank Sewall, "Daniel Hudson Burnham, A. M., LL. D.," *New-Church Messenger* (3 July 1912) 12. Sullivan, 286. Also see my "The Plan of Chicago as a Map of Heaven: The Influence of Burnham's Swedenborgianism" in *Influences Across Fields: Chicago Architecture Journal 10* (2002).

The Early Years
After the Great Fire and before the World's Fair

1. Burnham to Elizabeth Burnham, 24 November 1867, and 1 December 1867, Burnham Papers, Art Institute of Chicago (AIC).
2. Thomas S. Hines, *Burnham of Chicago: Architect & Planner* (Chicago: University of Chicago Press, 1979) 10–13; Charles Moore, *Daniel H. Burnham: Architect, Planner of Cities* (New York: Da Capo Press, 1968 [1921]) I, 14–17. In a letter to his mother, Burnham indicates he was already working for Sanford Loring and William LeBaron Jenney in 1867. Burnham to Elizabeth Burnham, 11 November 1867, Burnham Papers, AIC. Peter B. Wight, "Daniel Hudson Burnham: An Appreciation." *Architectural Record* XXXII (August 1912) 178. That is to say, there were no schools located within established institutions

of higher education. MIT was the first. See Mary N. Woods, "Training and Education" in *From Craft to Profession: The Practice of Architecture in Nineteenth-Century America* (Berkeley: University Of California Press, 1999) 53–81.

3. Donald Hoffmann, *The Architecture of John Wellborn Root* (Baltimore: The Johns Hopkins University Press, 1973) 5–6; Peter B. Wight, "Daniel Hudson Burnham and His Associates," *Architectural Record* XXXVIII (July 1915) 4–6; Wight, 1912, 178.

4. Harriet Monroe, *John Wellborn Root: A Study of His Life and Work* (Park Forest, Illinois: The Prairie School Press, 1966 [1896]) 44. That contemporary was Mrs. Henry Demarest Lloyd. Burnham & Root designed a house for the Lloyds in 1875. Hines, 25; Hoffmann, 247; Moore, I, 17; Monroe, 25; Wight, 1912, 178.

5. Monroe, 17; Sullivan, 287; Wight, 1912, 178. Much has been written about Root's design ability. By emphasizing Burnham's role I am differing with most historians but especially with respected Root scholar (and esteemed friend) Donald Hoffmann.

6. The remarks are those of Root's brother Walter C. Root, who worked in the office from 1879 to 1886. Quoted in Monroe, 117–18, and see also 120 & 114.

7. Monroe, 122 & 123. And this from the writer who, in her autobiography, called Burnham "one of those magnificent egoists who rule the world;" and who she said tried "to claim the credit for the firm's work." Harriet Monroe, *A Poet's Life: Seventy Years in a Changing World* (New York: AMS Press, 1969 [1938]) 114. My warm thanks to Scott Tilden for this volume.

8. Hoffmann, 53. A. N. Rebori, "The Work of Burnham & Root, D. H. Burnham, D. H. Burnham & Co., and Graham, Burnham & Co.," *Architectural Record* XXXVIII (July 1915) 41. This is not to say that Root did not recognize the importance of the plan as a practical consideration, especially in tall commercial buildings. In his "A Great Architectural Problem," *The Inland Architect and News Record* XV:5 (June 1890) 67–71, Root discusses the decision-making process of the tall building's plan. My interpretation of the article is that he is drawing on the experience of the firm. I also find parts of this article different from Root's other writings. See Donald Hoffmann, ed., *The Meanings of Architecture: Buildings and Writings by John Wellborn Root* (New York: Horizon Press, 1967).

9. Monroe, 122 & 123–24. The entire quote is worth reproducing: "Out of the long list of the firm's work, the buildings in the exteriors of which Mr. Burnham claims a share, by virtue of rough sketches embodying the starting-point of an idea, are the Monadnock, the Insurance Exchange and the Woman's Temple, a water-tower and office-building at the Stock-yards, the Montezuma Hotel in Las Vegas, the First Regiment Armory, St. Gabriel's Church on Forty-fifth and Wallace streets, the design (never executed) for the San Francisco 'Examiner,' and five residences, two of them—Mr. Hale's and Mr. Kent's—being of considerable importance. In the cases of the Insurance Exchange and the Montezuma Hotel, Mr. Burnham finds the relationship between his suggestion and the final design was slight, while in those of the Monadnock and the First Regiment Armory it was closest." Others simply credit Burnham with the Monadnock. Schuyler says that the Monadnock "is the individual design of Mr. Burnham." Montgomery Schuyler, "Great American Architects Series: Part II.—D. H. Burnham & Co.," *Architectural Record* (December 1895) 56. Also Rebori, 47–50. But see Donald Hoffmann, "John Root's Monadnock Building," *Journal of the Society of Architectural Historians*, 26 (December 1967) passim (hereafter, Hoffmann, *JSAH*). There he convincingly argues against the myth of the design as perpetrated by Monroe, 141. However, I think it would be an overreaction to remove Burnham from the design process entirely. Here there may have been the early sketches or critical responses by Burnham that the others have noted. But the subtlety and refinement of the design is, I think, undoubtedly Root's. See the discussion below.

10. In this, I am following the lead of Burnham's contemporaries, who credited him with having planning talent. Wight, 1912, 178.

11. Mary Walker died six weeks into the marriage of tuberculosis, but Root remained very close to the Walker family. Root later married Dora Louise Monroe, and by this marriage gained Harriet Monroe, the poet and later his biographer, as a sister-in-law. Donald L. Miller, *City of the Century: The Epic of Chicago and the Making of America* (New York: Simon & Schuster, 1996) 318.

12. Terracotta, like brick, is an earth-based material. To make terracotta, clay is mixed with water to form what is called a slip. Impurities are

removed, and then so is the water. The resulting paste is pressed into molds, then dried, glazed, and fired. As a malleable material that can be shaped by molds, terracotta is ideal for ornamental details. It is made off-site then shipped to the building to be installed. See Gary F. Kurutz, *Architectural Terra Cotta of Gladding, McBean* (Sausalito: Windgate Press, 1989) 133–37.

13. Hoffmann, ed., plate 6; Hoffmann, 19–24; Monroe, 130; Robert Bruegmann, *The Architects and the City: Holabird & Roche of Chicago, 1880–1918* (Chicago: The University of Chicago Press, 1997) 9; quote from Moore, I, 24.

14. Shepherd Brooks owned the lot, but Grannis leased it and had the building constructed. Hoffman 23–24.

15. The Grannis was rebuilt as the Illinois National Bank Building with two additional stories. Hoffmann, 24; Hoffmann, ed., plate 6; and Monroe, 130.

16. Bruegmann, 15, 66–67; quotations from Carl W. Condit, *The Chicago School of Architecture: A History of Commercial and Public Building in the Chicago Area, 1875–1925* (Chicago: The University of Chicago Press, 1964) 52.

17. Brooks to Aldis, 25 March 1881 and 23 July 1881, reproduced in Condit, 52–54. In his first letter, Brooks referred to the Montauk as an eight-story building.

18. *Piano nobile* is an Italian term indicating the location of the main reception and living rooms in a palace (palazzo), one story above the ground level. The term is employed here to designate large and important rooms on what Americans call the second floor. Condit, 55; Hoffmann, 24–27; Hoffmann, ed., plate 7; Hines, 49–54; Moore, I, 24–25. Root developed the first rail grillage footings, or floating raft foundation, for the Montauk.

19. Root quoted in Monroe, 259–60; Montgomery Schuyler, "Great American Architects Series: Part I—Architecture in Chicago" *Architectural Record* (December 1895) 8.

20. Barr Ferree in an address to the AIA convention in 1893, quoted in Carol Willis, *Form Follows Finance: Skyscrapers and Skylines in New York and Chicago* (New York: Princeton Architectural Press, 1995) 15; Schuyler, 8.

21. Aldis opined "Second class space costs as much to build as first class space. Therefore build no second class space." Quoted in Willis, 29–30. See also Daniel Bluestone, *Constructing Chicago* (New Haven: Yale University Press, 1991) 128–32.

22. Willis, 24–27; Bluestone, 132. Cooling was not air conditioning, which was a later invention.

23. The *caravanserai* is a Middle Eastern inn for traveling merchants (sometimes occupied by shops, warehouses, and exchanges as well) where a relatively thin zone of rooms enclosed the large open space of the courtyard. In the palazzo, the layer of rooms was thicker in relation to the smaller cortile. An illustration and definition of caravanserai appears in Joseph Gwilt's *The Encyclopedia of Architecture: Historical, Theoretical, and Practical.* Originally published in London in 1842, see the reprinted 1867 edition, revised and expanded by Wyatt Papworth (New York: Crown Publishers, 1982) 24 & 1167.

24. Hines, 54 Hoffmann, ed., plates 9–10; Hoffmann, 30–32. For a discussion of light courts see Bluestone, 132–33, 135, & 140.

25. The Phenix Building housed the western offices of the Phenix Insurance Co. of Brooklyn. The building was later the Western Union Telegraph Building, and the Austin Building. Wight recorded that this approximately one-hundred-foot long wall was the first truly skeletal wall of which he was aware. Wight, 1915, 8; Hoffmann, 64.

26. The Rookery was 179 feet by 167 feet; its court 71 feet by 62 feet. Hoffmann, ed., plate 31. In addition to the CB&Q, there were light courts in Boyington's Superior Block (1872), and Burling and Whitehouse's First National Bank (1881). Bluestone 132–33.

27. Hoffmann, 66–67; Bruegmann, 70–72; Hoffmann, ed., plate 31. The building was commissioned by the Central Safety Deposit Corporation controlled by the Brooks Brothers. It was a legal entity constructed to allow them to get around the law prohibiting speculative office building by limited liability corporations. See Robert Bruegmann, "Touchstone of Preservation," *Inland Architect* (July–August 1992) 50–55. The general contractor was the George Fuller Co. Woods, 157.

28. Hines, 57–59, gave Burnham credit for the plan of the Rookery; but Hoffman, 66–83, said the plan was Root's.

29. Schuyler, 50 & 53.

30. Bruegmann, 70 & 114–15; Bluestone, 140. See also Sally A. Kitt Chappell, *Architecture and Planning of Graham, Anderson, Probst and*

White, 1912–1936: Transforming Tradition (Chicago: The University of Chicago Press, 1992) 2, for another discussion of building hierarchy.

31. Unfortunately Frank Lloyd Wright's renovation of the interior (1905–07) has destroyed its original open airiness. Root's floor design has been reproduced in the latest restoration. See Deborah Salton, "Burnham and Root and the Rookery," in John S. Garner, ed. *The Midwest in American Architecture* (Chicago: University of Illinois Press, 1991) 76–97.

32. Condit described the stair as an ingenious cantilever. The hangers on the staircase we see today were added 1905. Condit, 63–65 and 64, note 46. Hoffmann, 83.

33. A double-loaded corridor is one that has rooms opening off both sides of the corridor. A racetrack corridor is a continuous one.

34. Wight, 1915, 8. See also Gerald R. Larson, "The Iron Skeleton Frame: Interactions Between Europe and the United States," in John Zukowsky, ed., *Chicago Architecture, 1872–1922: Birth of a Metropolis* (Munich: Prestel-Verlag, 1987) 49–50; and Larson and Roula Mouroudellis Geraniotis, "Toward a Better Understanding of the Evolution of the Iron Skeleton Frame in Chicago," *Journal of the Society of Architectural Historians* XLVI (March 1987) 39–48.

35. Hoffmann, 70; Hoffmann, ed., plates 36 & 41. The light court is now covered at the top of the building as well.

36. The walls of the first two stories along Quincy St and the alley are carried on columns. Root's grillage (steel rail and concrete) foundations are also used here, as they are in the Phenix and Rialto buildings. Hoffmann, ed., plates 31 & 36; Condit, 58 & 63; Monroe, 116.

37. Bruegmann, 71, cites Jenney's partner William Mundie as the source of Burnham's wish to use only skeletal construction. William Mundie, "Skeleton Construction, Its Origin and Development as Applied to Architecture" (1932), 43; manuscript preserved on microfilm, Burnham Library, AIC. I have not yet seen this manuscript myself.

38. Bruegmann, 70–71. Compare the Rookery to the relative evenness and framelike expression of the Rialto elevations. Hoffmann, ed., plate 21; Hoffmann, 41–43; Monroe, 116; Hines, 56.

39. The quotations come from Hoffmann, 67–68, and Monroe, 139–40. The historian's remarks are from Thomas E. Tallmadge, *The Story of Architecture in America* (New York: W.W. Norton & Co., 1927) 184.

40. Schuyler, 50 & 53.

41. Salton, 77 & 80.

42. Montgomery C. Meigs designed the building in 1881. Pamela Scott & Antoinette J. Lee, *Buildings of the District of Columbia* (New York: Oxford University Press, 1993) 183–86. This volume is part of the Society of Architectural Historians series, Buildings of the United States, of reliable architectural guidebooks written by scholars.

43. Root visited Paris in 1886, where he would have seen ferro-vitreous skylights and decorative interior ironwork in the 1876 Bon Marche, for instance. See Meredith L. Clausen, "Paris of the 1880s and the Rookery" in John Zukowsky, ed. *Chicago Architecture, 1872–1922: Birth of a Metropolis* (Munich: Prestel-Verlag, 1987) 168–71. See also Gerald R. Larson, "The Iron Skeleton Frame: Interactions Between Europe and the United States," 49–50, in the same volume.

44. Bruegmann, 70–73 and 480–81, note 26. The court walls of the Produce Exchange are true skeleton construction, where "wrought-iron girders carried the infill panels and fenestration floor by floor." Sarah Bradford Landau & Carl W. Condit, *Rise of the New York Skyscraper, 1865–1913* (New Haven: Yale University Press, 1996) 116–22.

45. Hines, 64, claims the Rand-McNally Building is "the first tall building in the world to be completely supported on an all-steel frame . . . [and] the first skyscraper with an all terracotta facade." The court was 68 feet by 60 feet in a building 158 feet by 171 feet. It was demolished in 1911. Hoffmann, 132–137; Hoffmann, ed., plates 82–83. See also "Federal Government takes space in Rand-McNally Building," *Chicago Tribune* (20 October 18??) from Clippings Scrapbook, Burnham Papers, AIC.

46. Burnham and Root designed a number of banks, but they were not the first to use this planning strategy for them. Burling and Whitehouse's First National Bank (1881) had a skylit ground floor banking room, with a light well above and a second skylight at roof level. It is the same date as the CB&Q. Bluestone, 132–33.

47. Contact with the client began in 1887, but construction did not commence until 1889. *The Architecture of Cleveland: Twelve Buildings, 1836–1912, Selections from the Historic American Buildings Survey, National Park Service*, number 12, 31; Henry L. Meyer, *Society*

48. *National Bank: Navigating Change* (New York: The Newcomer Society of the United States, 1994) 19. See also Samuel H. Mather to Burnham & Root, 22 September 1887, 10 October 1887, 17 October 1887, 19 October 1887, and 10 January 1888, as well as a letter to Jenney, 23 November 1887, Western Reserve Archive.

48. The building is 110 feet by 132 feet; the light well 56 x 36. *The Architecture of Cleveland*, 33; Hoffmann, 117–18; Gregory G. Deegan & James A. Toman, *The Heart of Cleveland: Public Square in the Twentieth Century* (Cleveland: Cleveland Landmarks Press, 1999) 9. See also *Society for Savings Building* (New York: Exhibit Publishing Company, 1891) and *Society National Bank of Cleveland, 1849–1974: 125 Years of People Serving People*. The floors were filled in across the light well in 1947–48 during a renovation that also included modifications to the east lobby, new elevators, and air conditioning. The interior frame was removed and replaced with new floor plates in the major renovation of 1989–1991 in conjunction with the construction of the Society's new fifty-seven story tower, at which time the banking lobby was restored. The glass ceiling of the banking room is now artificially lit from above. Cesar Pelli designed the tower; Gensler & Associates the interiors. Peter van Dijk did the landmark restoration of Burnham and Root's building. Deegan & Toman, 108–9; *The Architecture of Cleveland*, 32. The whole complex is now owned by Key Bank. My thanks to W. John Fuller of Key Bank for making these materials accessible to me.

49. "Press Release for Centennial," "Society for Savings Starts Second Hundred Years in Redecorated and Enlarged Offices," "Historical Notes on the Society National Bank Building," press release, contact, John Fuller, no date, 2. *The Architecture of Cleveland*, 31; Meyer, 18–19.

50. Much of this disposition of space was outlined in Mather's letter to Burnham & Root, 19 October 1887, Western Reserve Archives. The twenty-six foot height of the main banking room easily accommodated two levels. In 1922, the executive offices were relocated and the space opened to the lobby. In 1929, the banking room was rearranged.

51. The seven-story, H-shaped, red brick and terracotta building with a tower had an entrance court between the wings covered with a ferro-vitreous roof. Hoffmann, ed., plates 61–67; Hoffmann, 103–06.

52. Hoffmann, ed., plates 68–72; Hoffmann, 99–103; Woods, 127 & 159–60; Burnham to Margaret Burnham, 29 February 1888 and 3 March 1888, Burnham Papers, AIC.

53. Early studies show a steeply pitched roof in the chateauesque style with articulated pavilions. These different architectural expressions show the independence of exterior elaboration from plan type. Hoffmann, ed., plate 90; Hoffmann, 206–07; Michael R. Corbett, *Splendid Survivors: San Francisco's Downtown Architectural Heritage* (San Francisco: A California Living Book and The Foundation for San Francisco's Architectural Heritage, 1979) 205; Monroe, 142–43.

54. Shankland designed the trusses. Hoffmann, ed., plate 87; Hoffmann, 139–44; Moore, I, 29–30.

55. The other partners were Norman Ream, Eugene Pike, and George Fuller. Hoffmann, ed., plate 88; Hoffmann, 150–54; Monroe, 151.

56. Monroe, 134–35, 143–44; Hoffmann, ed., plate 95: Hoffmann, 193–94.

57. Hoffmann, ed., plate 93: Hoffmann, 196–204; Monroe, 140; Hines, 67; Moore, I, 26; Bruegmann, 106 & 108. Concern over its height led to some unusual rumors. "It's a Leaning Tower," *The Chicago Record*, 15 January 1897, Clippings Scrapbook, Burnham Papers, AIC.

58. The Monadnock had a protracted design process; first taken up 1884–85, then again in 1889. The building is 198 feet by 66 feet by 203 feet high. Condit, 66; Wight, 1915, 8, says Monadnock is the last building in Chicago to be built on a spread foundation of steel and concrete.

59. A pylon was an Egyptian gate set in a massive wall. Here I am referring to the shape of the pylon which was battered, that is, wider at the bottom and gradually thinning toward the top. A cavetto cornice was a simple topping to the wall, with a quarter-round concave profile. Monroe, 141; Hoffmann, 155–76; Hoffmann, ed., plate 99; Bruegmann, 118–20; Condit, 65–69. In addition to brick, the Monadnock had granite ashlar at the entrances.

60. Monroe, 141–42, cites the Monadnock as a building that was close to an original sketch by Burnham; Burnham's biographer Moore, I, 30, says the profession credits Burnham with conception of the building. Hoffmann, *JSAH*, 269–77, refutes this.

61. Sullivan was speaking broadly and was not referring to the Monadnock. Sullivan, in Roth, 343. See also the remarks of a contemporary

Frenchman who disparaged the Monadnock as not being the work of an artist but of a builder; quoted in Henri Loyrette, "Chicago: A French View," in *Chicago Architecture, 1872–1922: Birth of a Metropolis*, John Zukowsky, ed. (Munich: Prestel-Verlag, 1987) 129.

62. Moore, I, 34. Woods, 121; and see lists in Moore and Hines.

63. Woods, 119, 139–40, 142, 147, 149 & 155. The firm still kept its own job superintendent. The quote is from Woods, 146.

64. Wight, 1915, 3.

The World's Columbian Exposition and the Shift towards Classicism

1. Dwight Perkins ran the office during the Fair. Charles Moore, *Daniel H. Burnham: Architect, Planner of Cities* (New York: Da Capo Press, 1968 [1921]) I, 53.

2. Moore, I, 34; Donald Hoffmann, *The Architecture of John Wellborn Root* (Baltimore: The Johns Hopkins University Press, 1973) 225 & 230; Henry Van Brunt, "Architecture at the World's Columbian Exposition," *The Century Magazine* XLIV (May 1892), but cited here in its reprinted source, from William A. Coles, *Architecture and Society: Selected Essays of Henry Van Brunt* (Cambridge, MA: The Belknap Press of the Harvard University Press, 1969) 225. Hereafter Van Brunt, 1892. R. Reid Badger, *The Great American Fair: The World's Columbian Exposition and American Culture* (Chicago: Nelson Hall, 1979) 58. See also James Gilbert, *Perfect Cities: Chicago's Utopias of 1893* (Chicago: Chicago University Press, 1991). In August 1891, Gottlieb quit because of Burnham's close oversight. Burnham replaced him with Edward C. Shankland, his own engineer. Burnham already had replaced assistant chief of construction M. E. Bell with Ernest R. Graham. Graham had been working with Holabird and Roche in Chicago, and was recommended to Burnham when Root died. Badger 70; Sally A. Kitt Chappell, *Architecture and Planning of Graham, Anderson, Probst and White, 1912–1936: Transforming Tradition* (Chicago: The University of Chicago Press, 1992) 263.

3. Later Burnham's title was changed to Director of Works. Thomas S. Hines, *Burnham of Chicago: Architect and Planner* (Chicago: The University of Chicago Press, 1979) 78; Hoffmann, 230. See Burnham's interview with Moore, "Lessons of the Chicago's World's Fair: An Interview with the late Daniel H. Burnham," *Architectural Record*, XXXIII (January 1913) 38, hereafter Moore, 1913; and Burnham's transcript of the interview with Moore, Burnham to Moore, 5 May 1908, attachment; Burnham Papers, Art Institute of Chicago. A slightly different version is reproduced in Moore, 1913, 38.

4. Peter B. Wight, "Daniel Hudson Burnham: An Appreciation," *Architectural Record* XXXII (August 1912) 182. Hereafter Wight 1912. For the wording of Burnham's commission, see Hines, 92–94. The Fair opened on time but not everything was quite finished.

5. Harriet Monroe, *John Wellborn Root: A Study of His Life and Work* (Park Forest, Illinois: Prairie School Press, [1896] 1966) 197; Peter B. Wight had a "branch office on the grounds" of the fair. Wight, 1912, 181 & 182; William Holabird, in Wight, 1912, 185. See also Henry Van Brunt, "The Columbian Exposition and American Civilization," *The Atlantic Monthly Magazine*, LXXI (May 1893), but here cited in Coles, op.cit., 311. Hereafter referred to as Van Brunt, 1893.

6. Hoffmann, 192 & 223, fn 8; Hines, 77; Monroe, 224–25 & 235; Moore, I, 36; David F. Burg, *Chicago's White City of 1893* (Lexington: The University Press of Kentucky, 1976) 191 & 343; Laura Wood Roper, *F.L.O.: A Biography of Frederick Law Olmsted* (Baltimore: The Johns Hopkins University Press, 1983) 426–27; Cynthia R. Field, "The City Planning of Daniel Hudson Burnham," (Ph.D. diss., Columbia University, 1974) 67–68. See also Frederick Law Olmsted, "A Report Upon the Landscape Architecture of the Columbian Exposition to the American Institute of Architects," reprinted in *Civilizing American Cities: A Selection of Frederick Law Olmsted's Writings on City Landscapes*, S.B. Sutton, ed., (Cambridge, Massachusetts: The MIT Press, 1979) 182–91.

7. Van Brunt wrote that the buildings were grouped "in a formal and artificial manner at those points where their great size and necessary mutual proximity invited a predominance of architectural magnificence." Van Brunt, 1892, 227. Olmsted in Sutton, 189–90.

8. *Inland Architect* XVI (Sept. 1890) 14–15, quoted in Hoffmann, 232. A contemporary remembered that Root thought he knew who the contributing architects would be very early in the process, that many would be East Coast architects, and he was correct. Hoffmann, 230;

Wight, 1912, 180; Hines, 80, who also says that Burnham and Root had wanted it to be a national and not a regional affair.

9. Olmsted, after his initial involvement in the plan, seems to have delegated much of the specific and detailed work to Codman, who had greater knowledge of classicism and formal landscape design. Hoffmann, 225.

10. The other East Coast architects were Henry Van Brunt and George B. Post, both pupils of Hunt; and Robert Swain Peabody of Peabody and Stearns, who attended the Ecole at the same time as McKim. At later meetings, the architects agreed on a cornice height (60 feet), a maximum bay width (25 feet), and finally a color (white). The other Chicago architects chosen for major buildings on the lagoon were Francis M. Whitehouse of Burling and Whitehouse; Jenney and Mundie; and Henry Ives Cobb. Hoffmann, 233–35; Hines, 83; Van Brunt, 1892, 234; Moore, I, 46; and Moore, *The Life & Times of Charles Follen McKim* (Boston: Houghton Mifflin Co., 1929) 113.

11. Massachusetts-born Atwood (1849–95) had some twenty-five years of experience by 1891, and had worked for Ware and Van Brunt. In New York he had seen notices of Root's death and asked William R. Ware to recommend him to Burnham. Ann Lorenz Van Zanten, "The Marshall Field Annex and the New Urban Order of Daniel Burnham's Chicago," *Chicago History* 11:3 (1982) 130, 132; and her entry "Charles B. Atwood," in the *Macmillan Encyclopedia of Architects*. Atwood designed the Fair's Fine Arts Building. Because it housed works of art, it was fireproof and was the only building to survive the Fair. It was later used as the Field Columbian Museum; was reconstructed in the 1930s; and became the Museum of Science and Industry. See Badger 68, 69, 104; Stanley Applebaum, *The Chicago World's Fair of 1893: A Photographic Record* (New York: Dover Publications, Inc., 1980) 9, 75, 107; and Carroll L.V. Meeks, *The Railroad Station in Architectural History* (Secaucus, New Jersey: Castle Books, 1978 [1956]) 127. The quote appears in Hoffmann, 221, but it comes from Unidentified Recollection (n.d.) 9, Burnham Papers, AIC.

12. Montgomery Schuyler, "Last Words About the Fair" [1894], in *Montgomery Schuyler, American Architecture and Other Writings*, William H. Jordy and Ralph Coe, eds., (Cambridge, Massachusetts: The Belknap Press of Harvard University Press, 1961) 559 & 563. Hereafter, Schuyler, 1894. Sylvester Baxter, "Baltimore Municipal Art Conference: 'Metropolitan Park System of Boston'," Municipal Affairs, III, #4 (December 1899), 706, footnote; also quoted in Mel Scott, *American City Planning since 1890* (Berkeley: University of California Press, 1969) 44.

13. See Van Brunt's discussion, 1892, 284–88, as well as Hines, 126–33; and Moore, I, 95–113. Their effort would result in the Tarsney Act of 1893. In that context a senator remarked that the large private practices are "not only models as far as art is concerned but . . . models in administration . . . These great architectural firms in New York and Chicago . . . [have] numerous employees consisting of architects, artists, engineers, constructors, and draftsmen whose entire work is conducted with the most admirable system." Mary N. Woods, *From Craft to Profession: The Practice of Architecture in Nineteenth-Century America* (Berkeley: University of California Press, 1999) 118. McKim is the only one who, in advance, saw the ensemble in terms of urban design.

14. Arthur Sherburne Hardy, "Last Impressions," *The Cosmopolitan Magazine* XVI (December 1893) 198. Author of *Wealth versus Commonwealth*, Lloyd's remarks are quoted by Burnham in his "Uses of Expositions," 28, a speech given to the Literary Club, 15 April 1895, Burnham Papers, AIC. John J. Ingalls, "Lessons of the Fair," *The Cosmopolitan Magazine* XVI (Dec. 1893) 143. Van Brunt, 1893, 309–10. Thomas A. Janvier, "The Chicago Legacy," *The Cosmopolitan Magazine*, XVI (Dec. 1893) 248–49. Ben C. Truman, compiler, *History of the World's Fair* (New York: Arno Press, 1976 [1893]) 595, puts paid admissions at 716,881 and free admissions at 37,380, for a total of 754,261 fair-goers on Chicago Day, 9 October 1893. This far exceeded the big day for the 1889 Paris Exposition, which saw 397,150 visitors.

15. Wight, 1912, 182; Peter B. Wight, "Daniel Hudson Burnham and His Associates," *Architectural Record* XXXVIII (July 1915) 8; Hines, 119–20, 125–25 & 218ff.

16. Shankland had replaced Gottlieb. Burnham had left Dwight Perkins in charge of the office, but as Perkins did not get along with Graham, he soon left the firm. In terms of the partnership, Atwood got twenty-seven percent, Graham & Shankland ten percent each, and the rest went to Burnham. Hines, 268; Moore, I, 82–83; Chappell, 260–64.

17. Wight, 1915, 10; Holabird, in Wight, 1912, 185.

18. Van Zanten, 134; and Neil Harris, "Shopping—Chicago Style," in John Zukowsky, ed. *Chicago Architecture, 1872–1922: Birth of a Metropolis* (Munich: Prestel-Verlag, 1987) 142–44.

19. Schuyler, 59–61. Rebori, 62–68, appears to use some of Schuyler's words.

20. I think Atwood learned more from Richardson's facade strategies than did either Root or Sullivan. The articulation is not skeletal or simply trabeated like Jenney's Fair or Leiter stores. Van Zanten 135–37; Schuyler, 59. The diagonal view of the Annex, which its corner site affords, is acknowledged by the symmetry localized around the corner of the building. Compare with Burnham and Root's Counselman Building, Hoffmann, 40, where Root's windows are symmetrical on each facade independently but not around the corner.

21. There was just the right combination of construction and maintenance costs to rental income. The speculative offices were rented out completely before store opened. Economist 22 March 1892, quoted in Van Zanten, 134.

22. Van Zanten, 138. The building cost $3,350,000 in 1896 dollars. Promotional flier, c. 1896, Ellicott Square Development Co. (ESDC) files. Paul Starrett supervised the construction for Burnham. The general contractor was Jonathan Clark & Sons, Chicago. In Buffalo, Sullivan's Guaranty/Prudential Building opened in 1896 too. *Buffalo Express* 17 February 1895. Clippings Scrapbook, Burnham Papers, AIC.

23. Moore, I, 85; Van Zanten, 138; The steel frame was designed to accommodate another ten stories. Promotional flier, ESDC files.

24. The cornice was removed after a piece of it fell, and the exterior was painted. Unidentified article, 15 October 1971, ESDC files; Van Zanten, 138; "Ellicott Square: Celebrating 100 Years of Excellence and Commitment to Buffalo, 1896–1996," brochure, ESDC files.

25. Unlike the renovated Rookery interior, the Ellicott Square is pretty much intact. The current floor mosaic dates from 1930–31; and the glass partitions separating the elevator lobbies from the atrium are more recent. Reyner Banham et al., *Buffalo Architecture: A Guide* (Cambridge, Massachusetts: The MIT Press, 1981) 80; Promotional flier, ESDC files.

26. *Buffalo Enquirer* 26 March 1900 and *Buffalo Evening Times,* 9 September 1897, Scrapbook, ESDC files. The court was and still is used for community events. In 1898, the Immaculate Conception Church Bazaar was held in the court, and in 1978 the court held the awards presentation ceremony for the six-mile run sponsored by Blue Cross and the Buffalo Parks and Recreation Department. *Buffalo Morning News,* 13 November 1898, Scrapbook & Charles E. Rath, President of Blue Cross of Western New York to Daniel F. Hannon, Jr., 18 September 1978, ESDC files. In the 1970s, "Brunch with Bach" was held in court, as well as dance performances, weddings and receptions. Unidentified newspaper article, 18 August 1972, Scrapbook, ESDC files. When I visited the building in 2001, the court was being readied for an event. Statistics come from Ellicott Square Classified Directory, Business card booklet, 1 February 1899; Ellicott Square Business Directory, revised edition, 1 June 1900; *Buffalo Enquirer* 26 March 1900, Scrapbook, ESDC files.

27. The banking floor was fourteen feet high as compared with the eleven-feet ceiling height of the ground floor shops. *Chicago Times Herald,* 21 April 1895, Burnham Papers, AIC. Promotional flier, Statler publicity brochure, & *Buffalo Evening Times,* 9 Sepetmber 1897, Scrapbook, ESDC files.

28. "Catalogue of the Ellicott Square Law Library, Rooms 903–923," April 1897, ESDC files. Buffalo Law School students could use the library too. Ellicott Square Classified Directory, Business card booklet, 1 February 1899 & Ellicott Square Business Directory, revised edition, 1 June 1900, ESDC files. While floors three to ten were ten feet high, the club took advantage of the attic above to obtain an eighteen feet high ceiling and a skylight for its dining room. At the opposite end of the top floor was the large office workroom of the Western Union Company. *Chicago Times Herald,* 21 April 1895, Burnham Papers, AIC. *Buffalo Express,* 25 May 1898, ESDC files.

29. Such elevator service was thought to be equaled by few other buildings in the world at the time. Promotional flier; Ellicott Square Classified Directory, Business card booklet, 1 February 1899 and *Buffalo Evening Times,* 9 September 1897, Scrapbook, ESDC files. To get some sense of the size of the building, its vital statistics were also printed: 1,800 outside and court windows; a ventilating system with a capacity of 21,000,000 cubic feet per hour; forty arc lights; 1,524 steam radiators; 400,000 square feet of maple flooring; 2,000 office and room doors; ninety-two front entrance and store doors; over ten miles of baseboard; over fourteen miles of wood cornice; nine miles of chair rail; and twenty-five miles of door and window casings. It contained 6,576,100 cubic feet.; 447,000 square feet of floor space; and 316,822 square feet of rentable space. Promotional flier & Ellicott Square Business Directory, revised edition, 1 June 1900, ESDC files.

30. The tenant wrote: "When a firm has an office in a building that needs neither city, county, state, nor country on an address envelop, it is pretty good evidence that the firm is in either a very good or extremely bad location." *The Ellicott Square News* vol I, no.1 (March 1897) 1, ESDC files. Ellicott Square Directory 1931–32, 1 September 1931, ESDC files. The club was formed on November 18, 1900. Unidentified newspaper article, 18 August 1972, ESDC files.

31. Hale also commissioned the Hale observatory for his son George. Hale first manufactured hydraulic elevators, then got involved in speculative office buildings. Hoffmann, 177.

32. Hoffmann, 178–80; William H. Jordy, *American Buildings and their Architects, Vol. 4: Progressive and Academic Ideals at the Turn of the Twentieth Century* (New York: Oxford University Press, 1972) 61.

33. Carl W. Condit, *The Chicago School of Architecture: A History of Commercial and Public Building in the Chicago Area, 1875–1925* (Chicago: The University of Chicago Press, 1964) 110; Hoffmann, 180–84. These buildings all have a stable, reassuring appearance, especially around the corner, that I think the Tacoma lacks. See Robert Bruegmann, *The Architects of the City: Holabird & Roche of Chicago, 1880–1918* (Chicago: The University of Chicago Press, 1997) especially 82–83 for the Tacoma.

34. Jordy, 57, quotes Jenkin's article, saying this is the first building completely clad in terracotta, however, as earlier noted, the Rand-McNally Building was completely clad in terracotta. The 1995 restoration of the building with its cornice was done by the McClier Corporation. Annemarie van Roessel, *Daniel H. Burnham and Chicago's Loop District* (Chicago: Art Institute of Chicago, 1996) 4. "Chicago window" is the name given to a combination of three windows, a larger fixed pane flanked by operable sashes.

35. Schuyler thought that a "monument that 'will wash' is already pretty nearly a contradiction in terms." Schuyler, 58–59. The addition at the northern end of the Fisher Building was done by Peter J. Weber, a former Burnham employee, in 1907. Van Zanten, 133; Van Roessel, 6.

36. The site had been given to the city in 1839 by the federal government, with the provision that it was "public ground, forever to remain vacant of buildings." The city had sold the railroad a right of way in 1869, in exchange for shoreline protection. The Illinois Central built its tracks on a trestle some three hundred feet off shore. The area between Michigan Avenue and the tracks had been mostly water, until it was used as a dumping ground for the wreckage of the 1871 fire. Who owned the rights to the submerged land east of the tracks, out to the federally established limits of navigation, was the subject of the legal dispute. The case was not finally settled until the passage of the Lake Front Ordinance of 1919. Daniel Bluestone, *Constructing Chicago* (New Haven: Yale University Press, 1991) 33 & 187; *Chicago Park District, National Register of Historic Places, Multiple Property Documentation Form, United States Department of the Interior* (1990) E-11 & 12. And see Lois Wille, *Forever Open, Clear, and Free: The Struggle for Chicago's Lakefront* (Chicago: University of Chicago Press, 1991 [1972]) 71–81 & 82–89.

37. Burnham noted in his diary: "Soon after the Fair closed, Atwood and I made a study for the Lake Front, to place [the] Field Museum andArmory on the land and beautify the rest of the space with formal work in landscape." Burnham diary, 27 July 1896, Burnham Papers, AIC. Burnham to Olmsted, 29 May 1894, cited in Field, 307–08 & fn 16. Other individuals presenting designs were Washington Porter and Norman S. Patton. See Bluestone, 183–94.

38. All quotations concerning the meeting are taken from *Chicago Tribune,* 30 December 1894, 1 & 7.

39. *Chicago Tribune*, 30 December 1894, 1 & 7.

40. *Chicago Tribune,* 28 November 1894, 8; *Chicago Tribune,* 12 May 1895, 1; *Chicago Tribune,* 3 October 1895, 7. Bluestone effectively debunks the myth that Burnham was the originator of the lakefront idea, but I disagree with his conclusion that Burnham's proposals were thus necessarily derivative. Bluestone, 186.

41. The meeting was reported in the *Chicago Tribune*, which reproduced their bird's-eye view. The illustration appeared on page 8; the article on the front page which it shared with a story on the previous day's record-high temperatures and deaths from sunstroke. *Chicago Tribune*, 4 June 1895, 1.

42. *Chicago Tribune*, 4 June 1895, 8. Burnham and Atwood's designs are also distinguished by the way they reveal the park as an integral part of the city grid, and make the effort to have the effect of the park be felt further back in the city. Their proposal was limited to the downtown site. Burnham made no mention of a lake shore drive, yet he was already working on this as well.

43. *Chicago Tribune*, 4 June 1895, 1.

44. Van Zanten, 133. For severing the relationship Atwood received "in hand $5000.00 check of the company and assignment of the whole interest in and to twenty-five 2nd mortgage gold bonds of the Great Northern Theater and Hotel Company to which the firm were entitled as part payment for professional services; said bonds being in the sum of $500.00 each." Burnham Diary, 10 December & 19 December 1895, Burnham Papers, AIC.

45. Burnham, his wife Margaret, and her parents John and Kate Sherman, took the cruise together from 28 January to 31 March 1896. Burnham Diary, Burnham Papers, AIC. All quotations are taken from the journal he kept during the trip. Burnham Papers, AIC. Substantial portions are reproduced in Moore, I, 117–28, where Moore made small editorial changes. Moore also reproduces two sketches from the trip.

46. Burnham sketched a map the African coast, and when they landed at Alexandria, he was reminded of the "low, sandy shore" at Evanston. His travel sketches reveal "his preoccupation with the relationship between the waterfront and the cityscape, prefiguring his later interest in large-scale city planning." John Zukowsky and Susan Glover Godlewski, "Highlights of the Architectural Collections," *The Art Institute of Chicago Museum Studies* 13 (1987) 122. Plate 4 is a travel sketch of Algiers. That Athens and Rome have separate port cities (Piraeus & Ostia) should be noted.

47. "Reasons for Beautification and Lakefront," Speech (?), n.d., Burnham Papers, AIC.

**The Late Architectural Works
and City Plans**

1. "Reasons for Beautification and Lakefront," Speech (?), n.d., Burnham Papers, AIC. Burnham's handwriting is not always easy to read, so it is unclear whether, in the first quote, he wrote "the" or "this" ugliness.

2. Peter B. Wight, "Daniel Hudson Burnham and His Associates." *Architectural Record* XXXVIII (July 1915) 8.

3. Ellsworth was also President of the South Park Commission. Control of Chicago's parks was divided among three separate park districts. The South Park Commission wanted control of the lake front park and Ellsworth set about to get it. Some of the guests who attended the dinner were Mayor George B. Swift, George Pullman, Philip Armour, Marshall Field, and H. H. Kohlsaat, editor and publisher, at various times, of the *Inter-Ocean*, the *Chicago Times-Herald*, the *Chicago Post*, and the *Chicago Record-Herald*. Also present were representatives of the South, West, and Lincoln (northside) Park Boards. Cynthia R. Field, "The City Planning of Daniel Hudson Burnham" (Ph.D. diss., Columbia University, 1974) 308; Burnham transcript, Interview with Charles Moore, 10, Burnham Papers. Burnham's transcript of the interview differs somewhat from Moore's versions. See Charles Moore, "Lessons of the Chicago World's Fair: An Interview with the late Daniel H. Burnham" *Architectural Record* XXXIII (January 1913) 44; and Moore, *Daniel H. Burnham: Architect, Planner of Cities* (New York: Da Capo Press, 1968 [1921]) II, 99.

4. *Chicago Tribune*, 11 October 1896, 1 & 7; Burnham to Ellsworth, 15 September 1896, Burnham Papers. A "Cross Section of Burnham's Proposed South Shore Drive Below Park Row" was published on 29 March 1897; and a "Bird's-Eye View of South Shore 'Made Land' Following Mr. Burnham's Plan" on 5 April 1897, both in the *Chicago Tribune*. Clippings Scrapbook, Burnham Papers, AIC.

5. At this time the partnership with Graham was a seventy percent to thirty percent split. Sources differ as to when Shankland resigned, but all place it between 1898 and 1900. Moore I, 82; Wight, 1915, 3; Thomas S. Hines, *Burnham of Chicago: Architect & Planner* (Chicago: University of Chicago Press, 1979) 268; Sally A. Kitt Chappell, *Architecture and Planning of Graham, Anderson, Probst and White,*

1912–1936: Transforming Tradition (Chicago: The University of Chicago Press, 1992) 264.

6. Burnham won the commission in a competition of fourteen architects. Peter J. Weber was the designer. Drawing, Architecture Department, AIC; Burnham to Ream, 1 April 1902; Clippings Scrapbook, Burnham Papers, AIC.

7. A. N. Rebori says the exterior is granite; Rebori, "The Work of Burnham & Root, D. H. Burnham, D. H. Burnham & Co., and Graham, Burnham & Co." *Architectural Record* XXXVIII (July 1915) 69, 72 & 81. McKim thought the bank "if it is not built of marble, it ought to be." McKim to Burnham, 14 July 1896 and 15 November 1897, Burnham Papers, AIC, and partially quoted in Moore, I, 93–94. David Lowe, *Lost Chicago* (New York: Averel Books, 1975) 206 & 207. Frank A. Randall lists Shankland as the engineer and Graham as the superintendent, but no designer; and notes that in 1919 "a small blimp crashed through the skylight." Randall, *History of the Development of Building Construction in Chicago*, second edition, revised and expanded by John D. Randall (Urbana: University of Illinois Press, 1999) 165. The building, 168 feet by 178 feet, was replaced by Graham, Anderson, Probst & White's Illinois Merchants Bank skyscraper (1924), later called Continental Illinois Bank and Trust Company, now Bank of America. This building utilizes the sectional strategy developed by Burnham in his Continental and Commercial National Bank, discussed below.

8. The Senate Committee chose Burnham and Olmsted, Jr. They, in turn, selected McKim and later Augustus Saint-Gaudens to join them. The quotation comes from *Report of the Senate Committee on the District of Columbia, The Improvement of the Park System of the District of Columbia,* (Washington, D.C.: 1902) 12. Moore I, 129–84, Hines 139–57, and Field, 138–218. See John W. Reps, *Monumental Washington: The Planning and Development of the Capital Center* (Princeton: Princeton University Press, 1967) 92–154; Moore, *The Life & Times of Charles Follen McKim* (Boston: Houghton Mifflin Co., 1929) 182–203; Edward W. Wolner, "Daniel Burnham and the Tradition of the City Builder in Chicago" (Ph.D. diss., New York University, 1977) 211ff; *Historical Perspectives on Urban Design: Washington D.C., 1890–1910*, Antoinette J. Lee, ed., (Washington, D.C.: George Washington University, 1983); Jon A. Peterson, "The Nation's First Comprehensive Plan: A Political Analysis of the McMillan Plan for Washington, D.C., 1900–1902," *Journal of the American Planning Association* 51 (Spring 1985) 134–50. To contextualize Burnham's planning work, see Reps, "Burnham Before Chicago: The Birth of Modern American Urban Planning," in *The Art Institute of Chicago Centennial Lectures* (Museum Studies 10, 1983) 190–217.

9. Original emphasis. Moore, I, 142; Reps, 1967, 94–98. L'Enfant had been familiar with French examples and had consulted other cities as precedents, receiving his plans of Paris, Amsterdam, Karlsruhe, Strasbourg, Turin, Milan and other European cities.

10. One of these illustrators was Jules Guèrin, who Burnham would later commission to do the most important perspectives for the *Plan of Chicago*. Moore, *McKim*, 200–1, & Moore, I, 165–66.

11. The Smithsonian Institution's building had also been permitted to encroach upon the center of the Mall; it is absent from the proposed design. Much of the report centered on design principles for the Mall, and the enframements of the Capitol and the White House. It gave "detailed and elaborate treatment" to the "development of the Mall." The locations for new public buildings were "arranged according to a rational system of grouping," and monuments and memorials were "brought into harmonious relations with the general scheme of development." *Improvement of the Park System*, 17.

12. Burnham's case was helped by congressional appropriations for the construction of a tunnel under the Capitol to replace the on-grade tracks across the Mall. Minutes of the Annual Meeting of the Commercial Club, 25 January 1908, 57, Burnham Papers, AIC. Cassatt's sister was Mary Cassatt, the painter. In a letter to Moore, Burnham complained that the *Inland Architect* had implied he was using his position on the commission to get jobs. He reminded Moore that when they first met in March 1901, Burnham had revealed his connection to the Pennsylvania Railroad; that they had had conferences about a Washington station in 1900 and early 1901; and that he already had made many sketches: "I was working under a regular contract with the Pennsylvania Company for that Station long before we met." Burnham to Moore, 17 June 1902, Burnham Papers, AIC.

13. Anderson first met Burnham in 1894 when, as a young man, he asked the successful architect's advice on architecture. Burnham urged him

to attend the Ecole des Beaux-Arts. When Anderson returned to Chicago at the turn-of-the-century, Burnham hired him. Anderson was originally trained as an electrical engineer. Wight, 1915, 3; Chappell 274–75 & 29–30. Burnham wrote to his wife that McKim approved of the style and the manner in which it was used on the station, and thought the whole and the details "'very beautiful' . . . In short, he was enthusiastic, a thing with him most unusual, and you can imagine how much this does to settle and rest my mind, which I find has been on tension more or less for a year over this monument. His dictum makes me sure and fills me with content." Burnham to Margaret Burnham, 10 March 1903. McKim relayed to Burnham that Cassatt "expressed much pleasure and satisfaction" over the Union station plans. McKim to Burnham, 23 March 1903, Burnham Papers. McKim, Mead and White had the New York Pennsylvania Station project at this time.

14. The waiting room is 120 feet by 219 feet by ninety-six feet; the concourse 130 feet by 760 feet. Carroll L. V. Meeks, *The Railroad Station in Architectural History* (Secaucus, New Jersey: Castle Books, 1978 [1956]) 110, 124–25 & 129. Pamela Scott and Antoinette Lee, *Buildings of the District of Columbia* (New York: Oxford University Press, 1993) 140–42. I could not agree more with the authors' closing remarks, 142, with regard to the "space-destroying arrangement" of the station's most recent renovation. It seems to suffer from the Victorian syndrome, *horror vacui*. Unable to abide a vast, magnificent, open space, it is compulsively filled with retail opportunities. This grand public sequence has been turned into just another mall.

15. Burnham to F. L. Olmsted, Jr., 3 October 1901. The project did indeed require technological proficiency. The total area of station and shed is 750,000 square feet.; that covered by the building proper is 250,000 square feet. Burnham to Maj. J. C. Pangborn, 8 July 1904, Burnham Papers. Construction required the largest moving scaffold in the world. It was built by plastering contractors from Chicago who coffered the vault. See construction photographs, Burnham Papers, AIC. Also Burnham to Baltimore Ferro-Concrete Co., August 1903, asking for alternate bid on ferro-concrete beams instead of steel.

16. Burnham to F.L. Olmsted, Jr., 3 October 1901. Burnham was irate when the Senate Park Commission was credited for the plaza design. Burnham to Olmsted, Jr., 6 June 1908. The site plan is a pencil drawing. Architecture Department, AIC. The Columbus monument caused many modifications to the plaza design. Burnham to Col. Charles G. Bromwell, 23 November 1907. Burnham Papers. The sculpture, by Lorado Taft, was erected in 1912.

17. The Post Office was completed by Graham, Burnham & Co. Burnham indicated the drawings were nearly ready for bid in early 1911. Burnham to Sen. George Peabody Wetmore, 31 January 1911. Chappell 84–85, 4–7.

18. Sarah Bradford Landau & Carl W. Condit, *Rise of the New York Skyscraper, 1865–1913* (New Haven: Yale University Press, 1996) 301. The Fuller Company was the general contractor on many Burnham buildings, including the Monadnock, Marshall Field Annex, Reliance, and Frick Building (Pittsburgh). The Fuller Company constructed buildings for McKim, Mead and White, Holabird and Roche, and Louis H. Sullivan. See *Prominent Buildings Erected by the George Fuller Co.* 1893, 189?, 1904 and 1910; published first in Chicago, then in New York. The quote comes from Gregory F. Gilmartin, *Shaping the City: New York and the Municipal Art Society* (New York: Clarkson Potter, Publishers, 1995) 159.

19. Corydon T. Purdy of Chicago was the structural engineer of the steel column and girder frame. Carl W. Condit, T*he Port of New York: A History of the Rail and Terminal System from the Beginnings to Pennsylvania Station* (Chicago: The University of Chicago Press, 1980) 260. Jules Guèrin did a presentation drawing (August 1902) for an article in *Century Magazine*. Architecture Department, AIC. The Flatiron's dominance in the area was short-lived.

20. Dinkelberg worked on the Fair under Atwood. Zukowsky and Saliga, 73. Dinkelberg had worked in New York as a junior partner in the firm of Harding and Gooch, and may have been influenced in the design of the Flatiron by Bruce Price's American Surety Building (1894–96). Condit and Landau, 211 and 231–35. But I think that Burnham may have had in mind A. Page Brown's Crocker Building (1892) in San Francisco. See illustration in Michael R. Corbett, *Splendid Survivors: San Francisco's Downtown Architectural Heritage* (San Francisco: A California Living Book and The Foundation for San Francisco's Architectural Heritage, 1979) 29.

21. Landau & Condit, 303. Such oriels were common in Chicago tall buildings, but much less so in New York. Although the Monadnock employs such oriels, there the material and the detailing reveal the loadbearing nature of the wall, while here the oriels have the opposite effect. The oriels gave the facade, in the words of a contemporary, "a happy effect in perspective." The surface treatment, not necessarily valued "as ornament," provided "scale and character" making it "acceptable as a representation of texture." "The 'Flatiron' or Fuller Building: Architectural Appreciations-No. II." (October 1902) 233–41 in *The Origins of Modern Architecture: Selected Essays from "Architectural Record,"* Eric Uhlfelder, ed. (Mineola, New York: Dover Publications, Inc., 1998) 238–40.

22. Landau & Condit, 304, quoting Dorothy Norman, *Alfred Stieglitz, An American Seer* (New York: Random House, 1973) 45; "Architectural Appreciations-No. II," 236. *Prominent Buildings Erected by the George Fuller Co.* (New York, 1910) 60. Both shape and location contributed to the winds that whirled around the building, especially at its Twenty-third Street nose, and *Baedeker's* noted as much in its 1909 guide to United States. G. E. Kidder Smith, *Source Book of American Architecture: 500 Notable Buildings from the 10th Century to the Present* (New York: Princeton Architectural Press, 1996) 319. The winds were also the source of the old expression "twenty-three ski-doo," as policemen chased loitering men away from the spot that whipped up women's skirts. The ground floor glass prow extension was added at the north end while the building was under construction. Landau and Condit, 301. The simple extrusion was preferred in Chicago, as was the maximization of the lot. John Zukowsky and Pauline Saliga, "Late Works by Burnham and Sullivan," *Museum Studies* v.11, n.1 (Fall 1984) 70–79.

23. Annemarie van Roessel, *Daniel H. Burnham and Chicago's Loop,* (Chicago: Art Institute of Chicago, 1996) 10. For a discussion of this and other Burnham buildings, see Carol Willis, *Form Follows Finance: Skyscrapers and Skylines in New York and Chicago* (New York: Princeton Architectural Press, 1995) 49–65.

24. Hines, 271–72. Burnham was a principal owner along with the Atchison Topeka & Santa Fe Railroad Company, the Milwaukee & St. Paul R. R. Co., and Joy Morton & Co. The owners occupied six floors of the building. Burnham to Graham, 25 February 1909, to Carnegie Steel Company, 10 July 1903, to Paul Morton, 24 April 1905. Burnham was also a director of the Railway Exchange Bank. George Merryweather to Burnham, 8 August 1910. Mary N. Woods points out the ethical problem for the architect of owning a share of the building. Woods, *From Craft to Profession: The Practice of Architecture in Nineteenth-Century America* (Berkeley: University of California Press, 1999) 46–47.

25. Given the emphasis on white reflective surfaces of some mass, this interior has more in common with Wright's renovation of the Rookery atrium that it does with Burnham and Root's original. The light well above the Railway Exchange atrium has been covered at the top of the building, and the office floors opened to it.

26. See Peter B. Wight, "Daniel Hudson Burnham: An Appreciation." *Architectural Record* XXXII (August 1912) 183. The "goddesses of agriculture" in the Railway Exchange facade may refer to the angels in the cornice of Sullivan's Bayard (Condict) Building in New York. *Chicago's Landmark Structures: An Inventory-Loop Area* (Chicago: Landmarks Preservation Council & Service, 1974) 8. Sullivan also had an interest in Swedenborgianism where angels play an important role.

27. H. W. D[esmond], "Rationalizing the Skyscraper," *Architectural Record* XVII (May 1905) 423; quoted in Carl W. Condit, *The Chicago School of Architecture: A History of Commercial and Public Building in the Chicago Area, 1875–1925* (Chicago: The University of Chicago Press, 1964) 114. Desmond thought the obviously non-structural terracotta was too slender as a visual means of support.

28. Given his position as owner and architect, Burnham could exercise even greater control than he was accustomed to. He insisted upon approving all changes proposed by tenants, and subsequently reviewed and determined the operating expanses. He also dictated to the building agent how regular maintenance inspections should be conducted, and made requests as to the type of soap provided. See Burnham to F.G. Fisher, 28 May 1906, 10 October 1906, & 16 June 1909; Burnham to W.A. Illsley, 7 December 1903, Burnham Papers, AIC, and other related correspondence on the building and stock company.

29. Willis Polk was involved in the design of the First National; Dinkelberg in the Commercial National. Burnham and Root's

Montauk Block was demolished to make way for the First National Bank, which was a hollow rectangle plan type. The upper stories of the Commercial National were "C" shaped. Hines 293–98; Burnham to Norman B. Ream, 3 March 1902 & 1 April 1902; Burnham to Alderman E. F. Cullerton, 8 January 1902; Burnham Papers. Van Roessel, 11; Wight, 1915, 7; Rebori, 66–72 & 84–85 for illustrations; Willis, figures 54, 55, 64, 69, 71 for views and plans. The firm used the end bay pavilion strategy the Mills Building (1890–92) in San Francisco. The unfortunate ground floor articulation was used by Adler and Sullivan in the Stock Exchange (1893–94).

30. Burnham to Margaret Burnham, 1 February 1904, 23 April 1903, & 27 October 1902, Burnham Papers.

31. Hines, 162. Also Hines, "The Paradox of 'Progressive' Architecture: Urban Planning & Public Building in Tom Johnson's Cleveland," *American Quarterly* 25 (1973) 434; Eric Johannesen, *Cleveland Architecture: 1876–1976* (Cleveland: The Western Reserve Historical Society, 1979) 71–73.

32. The federal building site was already chosen when the commission began its work. See Hines, "Paradox of 'Progressive' Architecture" 426–48. Burnham et al., *The Group Plan of the Public Buildings of the City of Cleveland, Report made to the Honorable Tom L. Johnson and to the Honorable Board of Public Service* (1903). The text of the report appears as "The Grouping of Public Buildings at Cleveland," in *The Inland Architect & News Record* XLII (September 1903) 13–15. See also Moore, I, 182–83 & 201–04; Hines, 159–73; and Field, 219–37. Quote from *Inland Architect*, 14.

33. Unfortunately, later decision-makers foiled the completion of the mall. It is now rather shabby-looking, host to a miscellany of bus stops and shelters, and underground parking garages. A highway (I-90) was built between the mall and Lake Erie; and more recently a variety of object buildings have been disposed along the lake edge with no apparent plan. The saddest thing is that the mall is almost impossible to locate on modern maps and plans of the city, particularly those designed for visitors.

34. Bennett knew Pierce Anderson from the École, and at the time of the competition was working for George B. Post who permitted him to help Burnham. See Joan E. Draper, *Edward H. Bennett: Architect & City Planner, 1874–1954* (Chicago: The Art Institute of Chicago, 1982) 7–10. See also Moore I, 189–96, and Field, 238–46. The competition was won by Cram, Goodhue, and Ferguson's Gothic design.

35. Chicago Park District, *National Register of Historic Places, Multiple Property Documentation Form,* United States Department of Interior (1990) FII-8, FIII-11 to FIII-13, and FIII-12 (quoting the *Chicago Examiner,* 5 February 1904), Chicago Park District Archives; *Official Proceedings of the South Park District,* 27 February 1904, Chicago Park District Archives. Burnham and Root had done some earlier work for the South Park Commission, such as the South Park Bridge (1880) and the Washington Park skating Rink (1884). Hines, 372; Moore, II, 205. And Burnham had worked with James Ellsworth on the Lakefront park and parkway design.

36. Plans for two more were adopted, and two were still undergoing site selection. Of the fourteen, six were squares (less than 10 acres) and eight were small parks (more than 10 acres). *Annual Report of the South Park Commissioners, Fiscal Year 1904,* 5, Chicago Park District Archives. *National Register* FIII-12. Hines, 380, lists other small parks with buildings by the firm: Cornell, Davis, Hamilton, Russell and Mark White Squares, and Marquette, Ogden, and Palmer Parks. Omitted is Calumet Park. Burnham also designed a casino for South (now Washington) Park. Fuller Park is a late example. Burnham to Margaret Burnham, 3 May 1903, Burnham Papers.

37. Hines, 226. The committee was chaired by Charles Eliot Norton.

38. Draper, 10–13; Moore, I, 230–36 & II, 2–5; Hines, 174–96; and Field, 247–80. Daniel H. Burnham, assisted by Edward H. Bennett, *Report on a Plan for San Francisco, Presented to the Mayor and the Board of Supervision by the Association for the Improvement and Adornment of San Francisco* (Berkeley, CA: Urban Books Facsimile Reprint, [1905] 1971). See the "Introduction" by James R. McCarthy. Although dated 1905, the report was printed in the early spring, just in time for most copies to be destroyed by the earthquake and fire of April 1906. See also Robert W. Cherny, "City Commercial, City Beautiful, City Practical: The San Francisco Visions of William C. Ralston, James D. Phelan, and Michael M. O'shaughnessy," *California History* 73:4 (Winter 1994–95) 296–307.

39. *Plan for San Francisco, 35.*

40. And it is with regard to the San Francisco plan that there is evidence of Burnham's Swedenborgian beliefs influencing his theory of city planning. Bennett recalled that Burnham "interested himself in tracing the correspondence of spiritual powers and the municipal powers as indicated in the physical lay-out of the centre of the city." This was not seen as unusual, for as Bennett remarked, the "laws of spiritual correspondence were often in his mind." Bennett, Statement on Daniel H. Burnham, Bennett Papers, AIC; and reproduced in Moore, II, 170.

41. Hines, 190–96; *Splendid Survivors, 30–32.*

42. Burnham's immediate superior was W. Cameron Forbes, Commissioner to the Philippines and the nephew of Burnham's friend Malcolm Forbes. Burnham and Anderson left Manila for Baguio to spend Christmas there where it was cooler. Burnham to Margaret Burnham, 7 December 1904 and 19 December 1904, Burnham Papers. "Report on Proposed Improvements at Manila" and "Report of the Proposed Plan of the City of Baguio." The text of the reports are reproduced in Moore, II, 177–202, and in the *Proceedings of the Thirty-ninth Annual Convention of the American Institute of Architects* (Washington, D.C. 1906) 135–56. Typescript copies are located in the Burnham Papers. See also Hines, "The Imperial Facade: Daniel H. Burnham and American Architectural Planning in the Philippines," *Pacific Historical Review* XLI (February 1972) 33–53; and his "American Modernism in the Philippines: The Forgotten Architecture of William E. Parsons," *Journal of the Society of Architectural Historians* XXXII (December 1973) 316–26; Robert W. Taylor, "The Best of Burnham: The Philippine Plans," *Planning History* 16:3 (1994) 14–17; Moore, I, 230 & 236–45; Hines, 197–216; and Field, 281–302.

43. Burnham also recommended the improvement of waterways for transportation and the development of summer resorts. Moore, II, 180, 182, 184 & 187.

44. Moore, II, 197–98.

45. "Report on Proposed Passenger Station and Track Connections at Manila, P.I." (1906), Burnham Papers. "Daniel H. Burnham, Past President, A.I.A.: In Memoriam," *Quarterly Bulletin of the American Institute of Architects* XIII (July 1912) 140; Hines, 156.

46. Walter C. Kidney, *Pittsburgh's Landmark Architecture: The Historic Buildings of Pittsburgh and Allegheny County* (Pittsburgh: Pittsburgh History and Landmarks Foundation, 1997) 105; and Kidney, *Landmark Architecture: Pittsburgh and Allegheny County* (Pittsburgh: Pittsburgh History and Landmarks Foundation, 1985) 75. Franklin Toker, *Pittsburgh: An Urban Portrait* (Pittsburgh: University of Pittsburgh Press, 1994) 40, 49. Burnham did the First National Bank and Office Building in Pittsburgh (1909); as well as ones for Cincinnati (1903–04) and San Francisco (1908). He also did the Third National Bank (1904) in Pittsburgh. Barringer Fifield, *Seeing Pittsburgh* (Pittsburgh: University of Pittsburgh Press, 1996) 63.

47. Kidney, 1997, 245–46; Kidney, 1985, 166; James D. Van Trump & Arthur P. Ziegler, Jr., *Landmark Architecture of Allegheny County Pennsylvania* (Pittsburgh: Pittsburgh History and Landmarks Foundation, 1967) 49. The building has been well maintained over the years, ". . . and the modernization that is supposed to make so many aging office buildings look new and merely makes them look third-rate has simply never been visited on the Frick Building." Walter C. Kidney, "The Frick Building," *Executive Report* (June–July 1981) 16. My thanks to Mr. Kidney for providing me with a copy of this article.

48. *Pittsburgh Dispatch* 13 July 1902. Both the Frick Building and the Allegheny County Courthouse suffered when Grant's Hill "Hump" was lowered in 1911–13. The original first floor of the Frick Building is now the second floor mezzanine. Richardson's building was similarly affected but with more devastating results. Kidney, 1997, 245–26.

49. The lions (which used to sit at pedestrian level and now sit above the height of the doorway) are the work of Alexander Phimister Proctor who, with Theodore Barr, was responsible for the lions flanking the entrance of the Palace of Fine Arts at the 1893 Fair. Van Trump, 49; Stanley Appelbaum, *The Chicago World's Fair of 1893* (New York: Dover Publications, Inc., 1980) 75.

50. The description of the window comes from Henry Adams, "The Mind of John LaFarge." in Adams et al., *John LaFarge* (New York: Abbeville Press, 1987) 66. My sincere thanks to Walter Kidney for introducing me to this delightful quote. See also Henry A. LaFarge, "Painting with Colored Light: The Stained Glass of John LaFarge," in *John LaFarge,* 218: "usually represented as a giver of prosperity, the goddess was often shown riding on a wheel, to indicate the fickleness of fortune." The lowering of the ground floor destroyed the direct impact of the

Field, Cynthia R. "The City Planning of Daniel Hudson Burnham." Ph.D. diss., Columbia University, 1974.

Gilbert, Cass. "Daniel Hudson Burnham: An Appreciation." *Architectural Record* XXXII (August 1912) 175–85.

Gillette, Howard F. jr. "White City, Capital City." *Chicago History* XVIII, #4 (Winter 1989–90) 26–45

Harris, Neil. "Shopping Chicago Style." In John Zukowsky, ed. *Chicago Architecture, 1872–1922: Birth of a Metropolis.* Munich: Prestel-Verlag, 1987. 136–55

Hines, Thomas S. *Burnham of Chicago: Architect & Planner.* Chicago: University of Chicago Press, 1979.

Hines, Thomas S. "The Imperial Facade: Daniel H. Burnham and American Architectural Planning in the Philippines." *Pacific Historical Review* XLI (February 1972) 33–53.

Hines, Thomas S. "The Paradox of 'Progressive' Architecture: Urban Planning and Public Building in Tom Johnson's Cleveland." *American Quarterly* 25 (1973) 426–48.

"Historical Notes on the Society National Bank Building," press release, contact, John Fuller, no date.

Hoffmann, Donald. *The Architecture of John Wellborn Root.* Baltimore: The Johns Hopkins University Press, 1973.

Hoffmann, Donald. "John Root's Monadnock Building." *Journal of the Society of Architectural Historians.* 26 (December 1967) 269–77.

Hoffmann, Donald, ed. *The Meanings of Architecture: Buildings and Writings by John Wellborn Root.* New York: Horizon Press, 1967.

Jordy, William H. American Buildings and their Architects, Vol. 4: Progressive and Academic Ideals at the Turn of the Twentieth Century. New York: Oxford University Press, 1972.

Kidney, Walter C. *Landmark Architecture: Pittsburgh and Allegheny County* Pittsburgh: Pittsburgh History and Landmarks Foundation, 1985.

Kidney, Walter C. *Pittsburgh's Landmark Architecture: The Historic Buildings of Pittsburgh and Allegheny County.* Pittsburgh: Pittsburgh History and Landmarks Foundation, 1997.

Landau, Sarah Bradford & Carl W. Condit. *Rise of the New York Skyscraper, 1865–1913.* New Haven: Yale University Press, 1996.

Larson, Gerald R. "The Iron Skeleton Frame: Interactions Between Europe and the United States," in John Zukowsky, ed. *Chicago Architecture, 1872–1922: Birth of a Metropolis.* Munich: Prestel-Verlag, 1987. 38–55

Larson, Gerald R. and Roula Mouroudellis Geraniotis, "Toward a Better Understanding of the Evolution of the Iron Skeleton Frame in Chicago," *Journal of the Society of Architectural Historians* XLVI (March 1987) 39–48.

Lewis, Arnold. *An Early Encounter with Tomorrow: Europeans, Chicago's Loop, and the World's Columbian Exposition.* Urbana: University of Illinois Press, 1997.

Lowe, David. *Lost Chicago.* New York: Avenel Books, 1975.

Manieri-Elia, Mario. "Toward an 'Imperial City': Daniel H. Burnham and the City Beautiful Movement," in *The American City: From the Civil War to the New Deal*, Giorgio Ciucci et al. Cambridge: MIT Press, 1979.

Meeks, Carroll L. V. *The Railroad Station in Architectural History.* Secaucus, New Jersey: Castle Books, 1978 [1956].

Miller, Donald L. *City of the Century: The Epic of Chicago and the Making of America.* New York: Simom & Schuster, 1996.

Monroe, Harriet. *John Wellborn Root: A Study of His Life and Work.* Park Forest, Illinois: The Prairie School Press, 1966 [1896].

Moore, Charles. *Daniel H. Burnham: Architect, Planner of Cities.* 2 volumes in one. New York: Da Capo Press, 1968 [1921].

Moore, Charles. "Lessons of the Chicago's World's Fair: An Interview with the late Daniel H. Burnham," *Architectural Record*, XXXIII (January 1913) xx–xx.

Parsons, William E. "Burnham as a Pioneer in City Planning." *Architectural Record* XXXVIII (July 1915) 13–31.

Peterson, Jon A. "The Origins of the Comprehensive City Planning Ideal in the United States, 1840–1911." Ph.D. diss., Harvard University, 1967.

Pridmore, Jay. *Marshall Field's: A Building Book from the Chicago Architecture Foundation.* San Francisco: Pomegranate, 2002.

Randall, Frank A. *History of the Development of Building Construction in Chicago.* Second edition, revised and expanded by John D. Randall. Urbana: University of Illinois Press, 1999.

Rebori, A.N. "The Work of Burnham & Root, D. H. Burnham, D. H. Burnham & Co., and Graham, Burnham & Co." *Architectural Record* XXXVIII (July 1915) 33–168.

Report of the Architectural Advisory Committee to the Commission on Chicago Historical and Architectural Landmarks on the Central Development Area. Unpublished report. 1972[?]

Reps, John W. "Burnham Before Chicago: The Birth of Modern American Urban Planning." *The Art Institute of Chicago Centennial Lectures* (Chicago: Contemporary Books, 1983) 190–217.

Salton, Deborah. "Burnham and Root and the Rookery," in John S. Garner, ed. *The Midwest in American Architecture.* Chicago: University of Illinois Press, 1991.

Schaffer, Kristen. "Daniel H. Burnham: Urban Ideals and the *Plan of Chicago*." Ph.D. diss., Cornell University, 1993.

Schaffer, Kristen. "Fabric of City Life: The Social Agenda in Burnham's Draft of the *Plan of Chicago*," in Daniel H. Burnham and Edward H. Bennett, *Plan of Chicago.* New York: Princeton Architectural Press, 1993 [1909].

Schuyler, Montgomery. "Great American Architects Series: Part I. Architecture in Chicago [Adler & Sullivan]" and Part II. D. H. Burnham & Co." *Architectural Record* (December 1895) 2–48 & 49–69.

Scott, Pamela and Antoinette Lee. Buildings of the District of Columbia. New York: Oxford University Press, 1993.

Society National Bank of Cleveland, 1849–1974: 125 Years of People Serving People

Toker, Franklin. *Pittsburgh: An Urban Portrait.* Pittsburgh: University of Pittsburgh Press, 1994.

van Roessel, Annemarie. *Daniel H. Burnham and Chicago's Loop.* Chicago: Art Institute of Chicago, 1996.

Van Trump, James D. & Arthur P. Ziegler, jr. *Landmark Architecture of Allegheny County Pennsylvania.* Pittsburgh: Pittsburgh History and Landmarks Foundation, 1967.

Van Zanten, Ann Lorenz. "The Marshall Field Annex and the New Urban Order of Daniel Burnham's Chicago." *Chicago History* 11:3 (1982) 130–41.

Webster, Richard. *Philadelphia Preserved: Catalog of the Historic American Buildings Survey.* Charles E. Peterson, intro. Philadelphia: Temple University Press, 1981.

Wight, Peter B. "Daniel Hudson Burnham: An Appreciation." *Architectural Record* XXXII (August 1912) 176–84.

Wight, Peter B. "Daniel Hudson Burnham and His Associates." *Architectural Record* XXXVIII (July 1915) 1–12.

Willis, Carol. *Form Follows Finance: Skyscrapers and Skylines in New York and Chicago.* New York: Princeton Architectural Press, 1995.

Wilson, William H. *The City Beautiful Movement.* Baltimore: The Johns Hopkins University Press, 1989.

Wolner, Edward W. "Daniel Burnham and the Tradition of the City Builder in Chicago: Technique, Ambition and City Planning." Ph.D. diss., New York University, 1977.

Woods, Mary N. *From Craft to Profession: The Practice of Architecture in Nineteenth-Century America.* Berkeley: University of California Press, 1999.

Zukowsky, John, ed. *Chicago Architecture, 1872–1922: Birth of a Metropolis.* Munich: Prestel-Verlag, 1987.

Photo Credits

All photographs by Paul Rocheleau except as noted below.

Meigs, Montgomery C., 210n42
Merchants Club of Chicago, 177, 182
Midland Hotel (Kansas City), 50, 86
Mills Building. *See* D. O. Mills Building
Monadnock Building (Chicago), 10, 22, 56, *56–61*, 60, 86
Monroe, Harriet, 22, 53, 209n11
Montauk Block (Chicago), 24, 25, 215n29
Moore, Charles, 9, 208n13
Morton, Joy, 216n65
Mumford, Lewis, 11
Mundie, William, 210n37
Museum of Science and Industry (Chicago). *See* Fine Arts Building

N

National Fine Arts Commission, 148
New York, New York, 120, 122–28, 186
New York Edison Office Building (New York), 186
New York Produce Exchange (New York), 36
New York Times Building, 128

O

office buildings, speculative, 23–27, 34, 36, 54–56, 60, 141, 148, 150, 152, 154, 158, 162, 176–77, 202–3
   double-loaded racetrack corridors, 34, 55, 81, 189, 210n33
   double prime floor plan, 24, 81
   economics of, 14–15, 17, 25, 27, 34, 36
   facade strategies for, 152, 154, 203–4
   light courts and atriums in, 24, 25–27, 34, 36, 55–56, 73, 79, 98, 128, 202
   plan types for, 22, 24, 25, 36, 201
Oliver, Henry W., 148
Oliver Building. *See* Henry W. Oliver Building
Olmsted, Frederick Law, 63, 64, 67, 92, 99
Olmsted, Frederick Law, Jr., 213n8
Olmsted Brothers, 144
Orchestra Hall (Chicago), *140–41*, 141
oriels, 214n21
Otis Elevator Office Building (Chicago), 186

P

Parmelee Building (Cleveland), 50
Payne, Alina A., 217n4
Peabody, Robert Swain, 211n10
Peabody and Stearns firm, *64–65*
Pelli, Cesar, 210n48
Penn Station (Pittsburgh), *8–9*, *10*, 100, *100–106*
Pension Building (Washington, D.C.), 36
People's Gas, Light and Coke Company Building (Chicago), 186, *188–93*, 189, 192
   floor plans, *189*
Perkins, Dwight, 9, 211n1, 211n16
Phelan, James D., 144
Phenix Insurance Company Building (Chicago), 24, 26–27, 34
Philadelphia, Pennsylvania, 169–75
Philippines, 9, 144, 147–48
piano nobile, 209n18
Pike, Eugene, 210n55
Piranesi, 34
Pittsburgh, Pennsylvania, 148–62
Polk, Willis, 176, 214n29
Portland Block (Chicago), 23
Post, George B., 36, *64–65*, 211n10, 215n34
Price, Bruce, 214n20
Probst, Edward, 177, 216n66
Proctor, Alexander Phimister, 150, 215n49
Pullman, George, 92, 213n3
Purdy, Corydon T., 214n19
pylon, 210n59

R

Railway Exchange Building (Chicago), *12–13*, *17*, 128, *128–39*, 141, 142, *192*, *200–201*, *204*
   floor plans, *132*
Rand-McNally Building (Chicago), 36, 42, 212n34
   demolition of, 195
Ream, Norman, 210n55
Rebori, A. N., 216n78
Reliance Building (Chicago), 85–86, *86–89*, 91
Renwick, James, 21
residences, 23
Rialto Building (Chicago), 24, 86
Richardson, Henry Hobson, 148
   influence of, 36, 73, 79
Rookery, The (Chicago), *15*, *21–22*, *26–39*, *27*, 34, 36, 98, 195, 196, *199*
   compared with other buildings, 79, 85, 86, 128
   floor plans, *27*
Root, Dora Louise Monroe, 209n11
Root, John Wellborn. *See also* Burnham and Root firm
   death of, 23, 68, 86, 95, 203
   design talent of, 22, 34, 36
   early years of, 21
   marriages of, 23, 209n11
   partnership with Burnham, 9, 10, 11, 13–15, 21–23, 34, 36, 56, 64, 67, 184, 195, 203
   personality of, 22
   visit to Paris, 210n43
Root, Mary Louise Walker, 23, 209n11
Root, Walter C., 209n6

S

Saint-Gaudens, Augustus, 213n8
San Francisco, California, 9, 52–53, 176
   city planning in, 144, 146–47
San Francisco Chronicle Building, 53
San Francisco Examiner Building (unbuilt), 53
Santa Fe Building. *See* Railway Exchange Building
Schmidlapp Wing, Cincinnati Art Museum and Art Academy, *180–81*
Schuyler, Montgomery, 24, 25
   on Marshall Field Annex, 72
   on Reliance Building, 86, 91
   on The Rookery, 27, 36
   on World's Columbian Exposition, 11, 69
Selfridge Department Store (London), *168*, 169
Shankland, Edward C., 50, 53, 72, 86, 210n54, 211n2, 211n16, 213n7
   resignation of, 98
Shaw, Howard, 208n7
Sherman, John, 23, 213n45
Sherman, Kate, 213n45
Sherman Park (Chicago), 144, *144*
Silversmith Building (Chicago), 216n78
Smithsonian Institution (Washington, D.C.), 213n11
Snook, J. B., 21
Society for Savings (Cleveland), 40, *40–49*, 42, *142–43*
South Park Commission (Chicago), 143–44, 213n3
Southern Office Building (Washington, D.C.), 186, *187*
stained glass, *6–7*, *18*, *150*
Starrett, Paul, 212n22
Stevens Building (Chicago), 216n78
Stieglitz, Alfred, 122
Sullivan, Louis H.
   on architecture as business, 13–14
   architecture of, 68, 128, 212n22, 216n78
   on Beaux-Arts style, 10–11
   on Burnham, 9, 14–15, 18
   on form and function, 17
   on Monadnock Building, 10, 60
   on Root, 22
Swedenborg, Emanuel, 19
Swift, George B., 213n3